It's not me

Understanding complex trauma, attachment, and dissociation
A guide for patients and professionals

Anabel Gonzalez

Translation: Beatriz Morales and Brandon Lane Ferguson

ISBN Spanish Edition: 978-84-09-01361-6
ISBN English Edition: 978-84-09-06686-5

DEDICATION

For all patients who have gone through the Trauma and Dissociation Program at the A Coruña University Hospital (CHUAC) Psychiatry Department. This book was developed based on their doubts and our joint reflections as well as the various situations that arose throughout the therapeutic process.

For Ruth, María Jesus, Pablo, Belen, Juan Jose, Ines, Ana, Inma and Adriana, who, during their time in the program, helped me manage and evaluate the work in groups, and contributed with their questions and input to help develop and structure the interventions.

For my colleagues in the program, Marisol and Rosa, and most notably, for Lula, who was a co-therapist with me in the patient groups for a long time.

For Luis and Paloma, for their help with the text; for Beatriz and Brandon, for their thoughtful translation, and for Sonia, for her invaluable work on the English version.

Anabel Gonzalez

TABLE OF CONTENTS

Anabel Gonzalez

ACKNOWLEDGEMENTS

The most important contribution to this text originates from patients that I have treated throughout my professional life, and their efforts to recover from the experiences that they have endured. I was able to accompany many of them during their processes of understanding themselves and of changing the consequences of their experiences. Out of their doubts and difficulties, a pathway emerged for the understanding of psychological problems that result from traumatic experiences, along with areas to work on to help resolve them.

The theoretical areas that have been the most relevant in my approach are the theories of dissociation and complex trauma, which are, however, not referenced here in detail, given the informative approach of this book. A more in-depth description with numerous references to many authors in this field is included in other texts such as *Dissociative Disorders*, *Dissociative Identity Disorder*, and *EMDR and Dissociation: The Progressive Approach*, the latter two of which were published with my colleague Dolores Mosquera.

EMDR therapy opened me up to the perspective of trauma and dissociation. From this therapy, current problems are regarded as stemming from adverse experiences that our brain has not been able to process. These "unassimilated" experiences continue to condition our way of being and acting in the world, often without us even being aware of it. This basic concept is present throughout the book, where we will be constantly relating the present patterns of functioning to elements from the past.

Previously, my training was based on group therapy, systemic family therapy, and cognitive-analytic therapy for personality disorders. All these focuses taught me the importance of relationships, both in the development of psychological problems and the way in which we manage them.

In recent years the field of emotional regulation has come to fit together with work on trauma, attachment and dissociation. I have worked with my colleagues Lucía del Río and Ania Justo on researching the relationship between somatic and psychological dissociation, emotional regulation, and psychosis. Our reflections on these topics have also enriched this book.

Anabel Gonzalez

1 INTRODUCTION

External circumstances can strip us of everything, except one thing: the freedom to choose how to respond to these circumstances. Viktor Frankl.

Sarah suffers from headaches, which doctors claim are caused by tension. This makes no sense to her, because her headaches are not associated with any worrying situations, nor do they appear precisely when she gets nervous. Mark occasionally loses control. He doesn't have a bad temper, but there are certain things that trigger him and make him explode, and afterwards he feels very bad about what he has done. Lucy has suffered from depression her entire life, but her mood has gotten much worse in recent years. For as long as she can remember, she has tended to be a negative, pessimistic person who doesn't value herself at all. Mary has memory problems and forgets fragments of things that happen. Sometimes she finds herself doing something without knowing how or why it started. Sophie cuts her arms and legs in an effort not to feel what she's feeling, or eats until she is about to explode, so she won't notice the emptiness that consumes her. Kathy frequently feels strange, as if she were having a dream-like experience and operating in offline mode, like an automaton. Carol hears voices in her head that insult her and push her to do things that she doesn't want to do. Judith is the fundamental pillar of her household, the strong family woman, and always takes care of the problems of those around her. Dan lives in permanent anguish, tormented by constant memories that make him feel as if the past was happening over and over again. Peter believes that he has no problems, but his wife complains about him not being affectionate towards her, and she finds that there is no way to reach him.

What do all these people have in common? Their situations seem very different, and if they had consulted a mental health professional, they probably would have been diagnosed with diverse pathologies. However, their problems stem from traumatic experiences which occurred during very sensitive stages in their lives and which may have been prolonged and severe. Because of their pasts, the way in which these people regulate their emotions is also affected. As we have seen, each one of them has reacted to what happened to them in very different ways, and many of them have reacted in ways that are diametrically opposed. Some, like Sarah or Peter, are so disconnected from their emotions that they no longer perceive them. Others, like Sophie or Dan, live their lives overwhelmed by their emotions. Both extremes are a problem because they prevent them from understanding and modulating their emotional states, which would help them perform better in their daily lives.

Another common element these people share is that they are in permanent conflict with themselves. Lucy is constantly torturing herself, Mark tries to control his reactions and is ashamed of himself when they occur, Dan fights with his memories, Judith feels that she is never good enough or does not do enough, while Mary and Kathy can't even define who they are. All of them reject aspects of themselves: character traits, the memories that assail them, the voices that they hear, and their emotions. There are things that they do not want to think about, things they do not want to feel or do, parts of their personality that they do not identify with or do not want to be. These conflicts with themselves are very present in their lives and consume a great deal of their energy. Far from resolving their problems, the internal fight is a nuclear part of them.

Where we will see a great deal of difference in each of the cases is at the level of awareness of what is happening to these patients and the origin of their difficulties. In all probability, if they were asked, some might relate their symptoms to their circumstances; however, most would not be able to find an explanation as to why this happens to them. As we have seen, in some cases the person does not even believe they have a problem - it is others who see it. They may think that their experiences are unrelated to their present way of functioning or that they have completely overcome their past. All these aspects will be reviewed in the following chapters.

Viktor Frankl was a Austrian neurologist and psychiatrist who survived the Nazi concentration camps. Although certain traumas may not be as obvious as Frankl's, many people have gone through traumatic experiences that continue to deeply influence and affect their relationships with themselves, with others and with the world. In fact, since the great wars of the last century, the study of trauma[1] has begun to have greater importance at a scientific level. It became more evident that trauma can influence the development of psychological problems, which can persist for many years, and in many cases do not improve on their own. Specific treatments for traumatic problems began to be developed, and over time, the links between trauma and pathology have become clearer and better understood.

In addition to the impact of the wars, in recent decades, the study of family violence, especially towards women and children, has grown in importance. This is another kind of war, with bombs that no one else hears and wounds that no one else sees, but whose short-term and long-term consequences can often be devastating.

This book is about the psychological consequences of all these experiences, but mainly, as Frankl said, about our freedom to choose what we do with them. An essential element to making decisions is understanding the problems that we have, increasing our awareness of what is happening both within and around us, and analyzing the options available to us. For this reason, many of the chapters in this book will focus on the understanding of the consequences of adverse experiences in mental functioning. In addition to understanding, we must actively engage in making the change happen to us. Enduring extremely negative situations generates rigid patterns of functioning that need to be interrupted and modified. We must intentionally and actively break the inertia that binds us to places where we don't want to be.

Key

What do we mean by trauma?

There is no consensus among professionals regarding the kind of experiences that should be considered traumatic. Almost dying in a serious accident, being robbed or losing all our possessions in an earthquake, fire or flood are clearly potentially traumatizing circumstances. However, at a psychological level, these are not the most damaging situations.

The human being has an amazing capacity for adaptation and survival. Unlike other animal species, our way of coping with what happens to us has much to do with our relationships. Throughout the long period ranging from conception to adulthood, humans are dependent on their caregivers. We develop in our mother's womb and establish bonds of attachment which protect us from the environment and allow us to develop emotionally and physically. Evolutionarily, this is what has allowed us to achieve very high functioning levels as a species. But our biggest strength is also our biggest vulnerability, because we are highly dependent on the people who care for us as we grow. Even as adults, human beings always live in relationships. That is why nothing can traumatize us more than another human being.

The consequences of natural disasters or accidents can be severe, but the traumas of the interpersonal type are more harmful and produce more profound disorders in the identity and beliefs of the individual. These severe, interpersonal traumas that occur in the early stages of development, or that are brought about by intimate relationships, give rise to clinical pictures which have been included in the concept of complex trauma[2]. Although the term complex trauma did not exist as a diagnosis in international classifications, many authors previously described how these types of experiences may affect us[3]. In fact, it is this contradiction between a reality that hurts us and our tendency to resort to others that we find most difficult to assimilate. Some authors propose that the central element of trauma is the betrayal[4] by those whom we trust. As the social animals that we are, we grow up in groups which provide us security and protection, and we continue to form part of support networks in adult life. Damage that comes from the world outside those bonds can be expected. But when the very people that we turn to when we seek out care and support end up hurting or ignoring us, this falls outside the evolutionary programming stored in our brain. For example, if we have been in a car accident, the worst part of that memory may be the lack of consideration and support from the police when they arrived, or lying on a hospital stretcher and no one telling us what is going on; or if a family member is in the emergency room with a serious problem, our mind might focus on a doctor's insensitive words. When we expect to receive help from such an esteemed figure, especially when we are in a vulnerable position, any hostile gesture or lack of consideration can cause something inside of us to break.

Therefore, experiences of domestic abuse, neglect or abandonment tend to cause the most complex forms of trauma. Harm is caused to the most vulnerable individuals within the group that constitutes a home, the one place where a person should be able to take refuge from the outside world. Experiences such as living through a war, surviving a kidnapping or prolonged confinement, or living with a partner who physically or emotionally abuses us can also give rise to clinical problems which conceal a profound personality disturbance. It is not only the memory that can't be assimilated, but also the breakdown of our beliefs about ourselves, others and the world around us.

Some authors have also described the so-called hidden traumas.[5] They are small daily-life experiences that could be considered of little importance or "what goes on" in all families. They have to do with a lack of recognition, an inadequate response to the emotions of the other, manipulation and/or non-support in the sensitive stages of childhood. Many of these situations are associated with the concept of attachment, which is the search for protection in the caregivers who we rely on when we are children, and evolves in adulthood to define our interpersonal styles in intimate relationships. The healthy attachment style has been called secure or autonomous, and is characterized by a syntonic, balanced and coherent connection between child and caregiver. If there is too much distance between child and caregiver or excessive preoccupation (worry), this will be labelled as an insecure attachment. In cases of extreme insecurity and fear, a disorganized attachment manifests itself. Just as a secure attachment protects us from whatever we encounter in life, an insecure or disorganized style will interfere with how we relate to both ourselves and others.

The effects of these early traumatic events may be different, depending on the stage in which they were experienced[6]. When many serious adverse experiences accumulate and the bonds of attachment with caregivers are disorganized, this results in a psychological phenomenon known as dissociation[7]. Dissociation is a complex concept which still has not been fully defined and includes aspects such as difficulty remembering an event; disconnection from the body, emotions, and the environment; or various physical symptoms. For some authors, the most characteristic element of dissociation is the fragmentation of the personality and identity. People who have experienced serious interpersonal trauma are often in a constant struggle against themselves, avoiding the memories of what happened and rejecting aspects of their personality which they do not identify with. They may feel, think or do things that are quite different from what they would like to, they may feel strange about the way they function in certain situations, or they may live in permanent contradiction with themselves. They have not developed a unified image of themselves, and many aspects of their mental functioning won't be accepted, regulated or modulated properly.

Dissociative symptoms appear in situations related to more extreme and complex traumatization and disorganized attachment[8]. Memory lapses can occur in daily life or regarding past experiences. Internal or external sensations are perceived as unfamiliar or from a distance, and their behavior can appear automatic or mechanical. Many thoughts, feelings and actions are not recognized as their own and can sometimes be perceived in the form of voices. There may be both marked personality changes as well as rigid control of emotions and behavior. Some symptoms are manifested physically and can include paralysis, involuntary movements, heightened sensitivity or a lack of sensitivity, loss of senses such as sight and hearing, and many others. Some people have these experiences during a traumatic event. For example, they see themselves from outside their body during an attack, or some parts of the experience become obliterated. On other occasions, symptoms reappear long after the events that caused them; for example, they can arise in a limited fashion in response to experiences in childhood and manifest themselves more intensely and clearly throughout adulthood.

These symptoms are combined with more general manifestations of complex trauma, such as the profound alteration in a person's beliefs about themselves and the world, problems with the regulation of emotions and urges, self-destructive behavior, difficulties with intimacy, alterations in the perception of others, and idealization of the people who caused the damage, as well as medical problems.

However they are manifested, it is important for us to understand the relationship between present problems and the past in which they emerged. We must also try to understand why these problems persist, even though we feel anguish and want to change them. A feeling of being misunderstood and difficulty in understanding what they have lived through is common in people who grew up in traumatic environments. On one hand, they didn't have the feeling of unconditional acceptance that every child needs, and on the other hand, their environment was often plagued by contradictions or paradoxes, or perhaps no one ever explained to them what was happening around them. Because of these lessons, both in childhood and adulthood, they will have great difficulties understanding, accepting and providing a balanced response to their needs. Therefore, the main objective of this book is to help both patients and professionals understand why these problems manifest themselves and why they persist. Our introspection and ability to connect with others, which was initially designed to adapt to a hostile context, must be redesigned completely. We must learn to look at ourselves with new eyes. Our perspective towards others and the world must evolve and become more flexible. If we can understand, we can begin to change.

2 CHANGING FROM AUTOMATIC TO MANUAL

We all must continually learn to unlearn much that we have learned, and learn to learn that we have not been taught. Ronald D. Laing.

John managed to survive a war that lasted for many years, a war that had, in fact, started long before he was born. For decades, generations of his ancestors had been fighting without ever being able to say how the conflict began or why they continued to fight. That was the world he grew up in and until he moved to another country, he did not even know that a different place existed.

During the war he developed many skills. He learned how to find the least dangerous places but also - since no place was safe enough - he acquired the ability to sleep without really sleeping, always kept a weapon nearby, and developed a mental alertness that warned him about the slightest noise or movement. He also developed a kind sixth sense for people which helped him detect any gestures or attitudes to be suspicious of. Without trust, there is no possibility of betrayal. These abilities saved his life many times.

John was forced to become an expert in combat. He learned how to fight like no one else and had no problem getting into a fight at the slightest provocation. He thought it was better to hit first than to allow the other person to do so. He also knew how to run and as a result, eluded a group that had attacked him. He ran into the forest and stayed there for hours leaving his attackers behind. His greatest skill was his ability to keep completely still, frozen like a statue, barely breathing. His pursuers were quite near, yet they couldn't find him. He even pretended to be dead once, and didn't feel the pain when he was shot. When he was caught and held captive for months, he managed to go unnoticed with his head down, dodging direct looks. He obeyed all orders and even became indispensable to his captors by taking care of other prisoners. He went above and beyond in his duties and behaved as a model prisoner, which helped him avoid punishments and penalties. Once he gained their trust, he managed to escape.

He saw all these situations without feeling affected by them, and it happened so many times that he developed permanent anesthesia. He no longer felt pain, fear or sadness. His mind only focused on how to survive each day, one moment at a time. Suffering was a luxury that he couldn't afford.

John was only 18 when he boarded the ship that would take him to a different country, leaving the war behind. However, emotionally, he felt like an old man with no energy left and at the same time, like a child who had missed out on his childhood.

He had entered this new world, but all his systems for adaptation were meant for the world he left behind, and he didn't realize that he should have deactivated them. The sound of a car made him reach for his waist to search for a gun. When he heard loud noises, he would instinctively hide behind something. He was unable to interact properly with other people; when a neighbor greeted him in the elevator or when someone tried to start a conversation with him, he would react negatively. He appeared unapproachable to many people because his face always reflected tension and mistrust. Although this new world posed no severe threats and he no longer encountered dangerous situations like those in his homeland, he reacted with the same automatic responses that had often saved his life. A quiet conversation in a coffee shop, a smile from the baker, the park where people strolled carefree - these were all experiences that did not affect him. Life could not pass through all the shields that had so effectively protected him. The emotional anesthesia remained, covering up all these sensations, even preventing him from feeling a light breeze or the sun on his face. The things that activated his internal warning system - and there were many of these things - generated the only sensation that he was aware of: the one that warned him of danger. Looking someone in the eye always made him feel uncomfortable and would cause an underlying tension to build if the eye contact was sustained, and so he always avoided it.

Memories would occasionally flash in his mind, with intense and unbearable feelings that would sometimes also invade his dreams. Most of the time he managed to control them, to push them aside, but by doing so, he was always tense. This was burned into his memory as a child: relaxing can cost you your life. He had also learned that uncharted territories might be unsafe, so he followed rigid, set routines. Over the course of many years, he had assimilated many things that were vital for his survival, and they had become integral to the way he functioned. Although he knew that the war had ended, deep down he was still living through it, and his body reacted as if he had never left. He did not realize that he was free of it, in this different environment, and that the references from his past world did not work here. Nor did he realize that he was missing out on many things that were not only harmless, but also positive and valuable. John was drowning from the weight of the armor that had protected him so effectively. Now it was those shields that didn't allow him to live. He was walking through his new world using the maps of his old world, speaking the language of his old countrymen with his new ones. His emotional numbness was so powerful that it wouldn't allow him to realize what was happening to him, and things weren't getting better just by letting time pass. We can only change the things of which we are aware. When going through a difficult situation, our system dedicates itself to overcoming the problem. If the problem in question can't be resolved with the resources we have at that moment, we focus on just getting through it. If the problem becomes too overwhelming, we will settle for remaining on our feet and moving forward. This process is mostly automatic and is even more so when we are faced with situations where we perceive a threat, because there is no time to stop and analyze. Survival becomes the top priority, and we operate at the level of instinctual reaction.

A soldier on the battlefield depends entirely on his basic survival skills. He must be alert, prioritize the detection of threats and hone his defensive systems. Amid danger, he should act before thinking, and do so successfully. In these reactions, we are not much different from any other species that would struggle to survive in the wild. In fact, these reactions are activated by the most primitive parts of our brain, parts that we share with less-evolved species such as reptiles. When faced with a threat, this is the fastest and most effective way of dealing with it. The problem occurs when these automatic responses are activated for long periods of time and become regular patterns. Over time, these patterns end up being activated in situations for which they were not designed. We react to harmless or very minor situations as if we were being faced with life-threatening ones. In these situations, we are always in high-alert mode and unnecessarily deplete our resources. This is equivalent to having an alarm in our house that is tripped every time a fly comes through a window: is this alarm actually protecting us from possible threats?

Experiencing a war is one of those serious interpersonal traumatic situations that can give way to complex traumatization and dissociation symptoms. However, this is not the only type of war in which humans are involved. Perhaps the most terrible battle is that of children who grow up in a hostile family environment. These adverse contexts are not only related to physical or sexual abuse but also to caregivers who are depressed, ill or are unable to understand or care for the children that depend on them. When a mother experiences a major trauma during the first two years following the birth of her child[9], the bond with her child can be severely damaged and affect the child's subsequent psychological development.

Furthermore, the characteristics of the human mind introduce other factors that increase the complexity of the situation. Let's look back on John the soldier and see how he deploys a wide range of defensive systems. These systems are activated according to each circumstance and are adjusted to the needs of that specific moment. He will fight an opponent if he is equally armed, and if he can't fight, he will flee. In the wild, animals do the same. A bear and a lion could fight, as their strength is comparable. Once engaged in a fight, if the lion were to take the lead, the bear would not feel ashamed to run away. However, humans would most likely feel ashamed, despite knowing that escaping was their best chance at survival. Our beliefs as well as our social and moral standards can negatively influence our ability to make sense of a situation where we did not confront someone or fight, and this could make us feel cowardly or bad about ourselves.

But the defensive instinct is not just limited to fight or flight. Both systems involve action, but what happens when neither option is available? How can we protect ourselves when a predator attacks us and there is nowhere to run? In nature, again, everything is simpler. In a lion's pride, the rest bow down and submit, unless they grow strong enough to confront the dominant male. No cub would ever attempt this. Nonetheless, if, as children, we were threatened by a teacher, an older child or a member of our family, we might feel ashamed for lowering our heads and not looking the abuser in the eyes, two tactics which happen to be very useful for surviving in such situations. Our body chooses the reaction that best protects us in each situation from its instinctive memory. But our thoughts don't forgive us for this choice and reproach us because "we haven't done enough." This belief can stay with us our whole life and influence us in many ways.

Lastly, in life-or-death situations, ones where there are no options, such as a predator cornering its prey, many animals freeze up and enter a state of apparent death, which discourages the attacker. Predators have learned through evolution that motionless prey must be passed by, as it might already be dead and is therefore too risky to eat, due to decay. For that reason, when in doubt, remaining still can be essential to our survival, and our body and our brain know this. This same survival instinct saved Soldier John. But when we submit to those who humiliate us, not reacting at all might not seem like the best option. We learn from children's stories and films that the epic heroes are not those who are paralyzed by fear or bow their head, but instead are the ones who win against all odds. Or even worse, they are the admirable ones who die in battle, because they put their ideals ahead of the fundamental logic of survival. Humans tend to introduce changes in their natural systems that sometimes do not work out, but nature is wiser and simpler. If while reading this chapter, we ask ourselves, "Why didn't I fight back that time to defend myself?" the answer will most likely be, "Because my body knew what it had to do better than I did." Evolution has taught our species that often times, not taking action is better, that attacking is not always the best form of self-defense, but rather, remaining completely still is. It might be difficult for someone who has lived through an overwhelming situation which hindered their ability to react or paralyzed them to understand that by not doing anything, they are actually protecting themselves.

As we mentioned before, the skills needed for survival do not fit in our everyday lives. It is not easy to reprogram your mental and emotional system after having to spend so much time on self-preservation. The tendency to move forward and go through the motions, to fix our past by not dwelling on it, can be very powerful. At one point in time, doing so was our salvation, and we are unaware that once we reach land after our ship has sunk, the board that we clung to saved us from drowning, now has become unnecessary or cumbersome. If we take that lifeline with us to breakfast, to work or to bed, instead of being a solution, it will become a problem for us. Applying a system that is effective in a very specific context to all kinds of situations renders it ineffective or may produce a short-term gain that will have negative consequences in the long run. In addition, disconnection which helps us stay standing makes us partially or completely unaware of the fact that we are experiencing disconnection. It is common for psychological or medical symptoms, which are seemingly unrelated to the previous history, to appear later. Even when people understand the source of their problem, they wonder if it is worth engaging in a long process of therapy that involves bringing up the difficult, painful past, when what they really want is not to think about it anymore.

Another repercussion of persistent adverse situations is that these instinctive defensive systems, by becoming automatic and remaining active for long periods of time, are activated indiscriminately. Therefore, they may appear later in situations where they do not fit. We are adults facing someone with similar strength, or we have options to get out of a situation, but our system no longer knows how to choose. Our mental and emotional system will always resort to responses that worked at that time, even if they are no longer useful or prove counterproductive. In any case, they continue to be attempts at reaction, ones that our body sets in motion.

The reality is that if we never stop to heal our wounds, they will remain open, and the pain will stay within us forever. Our body will continue to be on alert, because the news that the danger is over has not reached our inner self. Protection systems will be blocked and will react in a set way that is inappropriate to the situation at hand. The emotional anesthesia which has protected us from pain will make us think that we are over it or that it wasn't so important. We may believe that getting back to normal functioning is too difficult, that reconnecting with those deeply buried emotions and feelings involves unnecessary suffering. But not doing so is tantamount to knowing that we have a landmine in our garden. We believe that trying to avoid the spot where the landmine is will be enough, but one day, we could trip and fall on it. Although this may not happen, we can never really enjoy our garden.

3 RELEARNING TO FEEL

Between me and life is a faint glass. No matter how sharply I see and understand life, I cannot touch it. Fernando Pessoa.

When we get injured we often don't realize it at the time, but only later, once we have stopped the activity that we are performing and redirect our attention to see how we are. If the damage is something that continues over time, paying attention to how we feel is a luxury we can't afford, and disconnection becomes a habitual pattern of functioning. The same thing happens in the context of interpersonal problems and, on top of that, it is common in problematic environments where those around us don't realize how we feel or can't help us understand our reactions. A lack of attunement with our environment further heightens our disconnection.

Even when people are apparently overwhelmed by intense emotions, they may have difficulty accessing or tolerating some specific emotions. A child growing up in a family with high levels of violence is probably incapable of adequately managing his own *rage*, although he can take two opposing routes. One is to function impulsively, due to a lack of control of that anger; if something activates this rage, there is no stopping it. The other is an attempt to contain or bury this range of emotions, which leads to difficulties in saying things firmly, being able to say no or asking for what he needs. When the primary caregiver is depressed, the child may not manifest his own *sadness*, and if he notices it, the sadness that he sees in his mother or father's eyes reminds him of the painful distance that it creates with that figure. A sense of *shame* or *disgust* that the person can't disclose may lead to active avoidance of these emotions.

It's not only negative emotions that may be avoided or suppressed. Pleasure or happiness can also be feared or self-censored by the individual, because they are very alien to his life experiences, and because he feels that he is not worthy of them. Sometimes pleasant shared moments with caregivers in the early stages of life were absent, maybe because they were ill or because they themselves didn't enjoy things. In the latter case, positive feelings are awkward, and they are often a reminder of something that people feel that they should have had but didn't.

Emotions and physical sensations are our sensors. Numbing them cancels out our references of what is happening and how it affects us, about what we need and how to get it. We are going in blind, with no access to our intuition, and operating based only on the instruction manual of logical reasoning. This reasoning is also very distorted by the same beliefs that were generated by the traumatic contexts that caused the disconnection in the first place.

An important part of the recovery process is reconciling our emotions and realizing that we have resources to regulate them. Emotions are neither good nor bad; each one of them has a vital function, and when they work in concert, we can perform better in different situations. Sometimes it can be difficult for us to understand what certain emotions are good for, especially the unpleasant ones, but none of them would exist if they did not fulfil an essential function for human beings. So let's look at the different types of emotions and feelings - elements that are more complex than emotions - and their main functions.

What is fear for?

Fear protects us. Thanks to fear, our body is triggered to react to danger. The fear response is automatic and keeps us safe; it ensures that we escape from a threat even before we stop to think about it. When our fear is proportionate to the situation in front of us, it is an important resource.

Fear becomes a problem when it is constantly triggered by anything and everything. This happens sometimes because we literally "strike fear into our heart." If we are faced with a situation that scares us, but there is no way of getting out of it, we can't relieve this reaction of fear. When we have a scare and the danger is over, sometimes we tremble, cry or faint: this way the body "gets rid of" the fear and can move on to another emotional state. In situations where there is no way out, this relief can't happen, and the fear reaction gets blocked and is later reactivated in similar situations. It can also lead to a state of permanent alert, which keeps us in a constant state of tension, without being able to relax or rest.

What is rage for?

Rage is an emotion that gets bad press, but it has a lot to do with our survival instinct. Along with fear, these are the two reactions of active protection, which are first put in place at an instinctive level. If our opponent is stronger than us, our fight reaction is blocked by the body automatically. A dog can fight with a cat but will run from a lion. This rage, an emotion which is meant to be released to combat a threat, gets "stuck inside" and can become a symptom of different disorders.

In many cases, this blocked rage is also rejected when, for example, we have lived in close contact with a very violent person who we constantly witnessed lose control and poorly channel their rage. We may think that it is rage itself - and not what those people did with it - that is evil. We can say, "I don't want to be like him," or "I don't want to feel this." This rage that we don't let out in a healthy way turns against us and becomes self-reproach or self-rejection. By never allowing ourselves to feel and show our rage, we are also much more vulnerable, unable to say "no" or to ask for what we need, which feeds the increasing cycle of our hidden rage.

What is affection for?

Affection is more complex than a basic emotion. The tendency to establish an emotional relationship with others is innate in human beings. But when our first bonds are problematic, tinged by concern or characterized by absence or distance, loving someone can be experienced as dangerous or make us feel unsafe. We may avoid connecting with others or feel awkward when a relationship becomes too close. Engaging with others can feel distressing and generate suffering, or we can avoid intimacy by telling ourselves that we don't need to feel love or affection for anyone.

As previously described, feeling "positive" emotions can be more difficult than noticing the "negative" ones. Our first experiences with positive emotions were the interactions with our caregivers in childhood, including sharing positive affection, laughing and playing. From this basis we may be familiar with emotions related to affection and joy, but they may be experienced as foreign and uncomfortable if they were not often present. If we lack these emotions as children, then as adults we may feel a desperate need for affection and ask our current relationships to give us "everything that we didn't have," instead of what is reasonable. This leads to disproportionate reactions and creates many problems in relationships.

What is sadness for?

Human beings are social animals by nature. We live in groups and connect through networks of relationships. Children need their caregivers for many years, and therefore early bonds are crucial for growing up in a healthy way. This connection is also enhanced by a feeling we experience when we face losing one of the figures for which we feel affection: sadness. If we did not feel sadness when we lost someone or something, we would not remain attached to people or things. In the same way, if we did not experience hunger, we wouldn't look for food. Sadness, although painful at times, is important to the functioning and survival of individuals and communities. To put it another way: it is a kind of "relationship glue."

This emotion - like others - tends to self-regulate if we let it flow and integrate with the rest of our emotions. Sadness functions like a river which, by itself, knows how to reach the sea. If humans intervene, by building levees and canals, the likelihood of a heavy downpour causing the river to overflow its banks and destroy everything in its path is far greater. It's no use closing off the reservoir floodgates to avoid a deluge: this only complicates the situation further by letting so much water build up that when the dam finally bursts, the consequences are far more destructive. When we feel sadness, and then rage by feeling this emotion, the rage does not let the sadness flow out and pushes it back in again. What we don't let out stays inside us; we may not realize it, but buried emotions always take their toll.

What is joy for?

Joy is energy, and it has to do with hopeful anticipation, with the desire to do things. Having good moments is a kind of emotional nutrition that is as necessary as food. Despite its clearly positive nature, not everyone feels comfortable experiencing this emotion. Sometimes the thought "After something good always comes something very bad" or the idea of "I don't deserve to be happy," appears like a ghost which muddies the good times and makes them generate discomfort.

Some people feel that they can only devote their time to doing useful tasks or dealing with others' problems. Doing things without any purpose or that are simply pleasant for them is something that is not permitted, since it produces guilt or discomfort. Again, the survival system was meant to focus on carrying out tasks to perfection, to feeling control or trying - usually without succeeding - to meet the demands of those who are around us. We can devote ourselves to taking care of others without being cared for by others. As we have said, it is difficult for us to abandon old patterns.

What is guilt for?

Guilt is more a feeling than a basic emotion, and like the previous elements, it also has a healthy purpose. Healthy guilt is called responsibility and is what allows us to learn from our mistakes and correct them. For this to function properly, it must be proportionate to the situation. If we have accumulated too much of it, we will feel too guilty, even in situations where the greater responsibility lies with others rather than with us. When this happens, instead of learning from our mistakes, we get blocked and we sink.

Many times, when we blame ourselves for things from the past, we cheat. We don't place enough value on what we could have done considering what we knew at that time, the options that were within our reach, our emotional state, or our age. We say, "If I could go back to that situation, I would have done things completely different," but it's important to notice that we now have keys that we didn't have back then. At the time, we couldn't see the future, we knew what we knew, and we were the way we were. We did what *we could with what we had at the time.* A fair judgment must take this into account. We must also be aware that, since the time machine has not been invented, no matter how much we retrace our steps, we can't change the way things happened. Healthy guilt shouldn't hammer away at wounds, but rather make it so we can learn from experiences and mistakes to improve future decisions.

It is important for us to be comfortable with the feeling of guilt, otherwise we won't be able to have a complete understanding of all these issues. If we can't tolerate this emotion, we will see ourselves in two opposing situations, both of which are problematic: we can either feel guilty about everything or refuse to accept responsibility for anything.

What is shame for?

Shame is an emotion that helps us adapt our behavior to fit with the group to which we belong. We feel shame when we do something that we perceive as inappropriate or that may expose us to the reproach of others. Without a sense of shame, we would behave inappropriately and be unaware of the effect of our behavior on others. If we are comfortable with this emotion, we won't try to escape from it. Even when something embarrasses us, if we go ahead with it, the sensation of shame will diminish and eventually disappear. In this sense it works like fear and anxiety, which are more intense in new situations in order to activate our body and our attention, and sharpen our response, and reduce when the activity is repeated and familiar. Shame emerges when we are faced with something new so that our new behavior fits in with the social context where we find ourselves.

Complications arise when we are anguished over feeling shame, or when we try to avoid it, because then the process of habituation that leads to its diminishing and disappearing can't occur. Shame then accumulates inside of us, becoming more and more intense, and blocks our ability to process the experience; this may have a strong influence on our overall functioning.

What is worry for?

Anticipating what is going to happen and the problems that we might encounter is useful so that we're not caught off guard and have a plan ready. We can come up with different possible scenarios and imagine solutions for each of them. So far, everything is fine and very useful. The problem occurs when concern turns into worry, when we start imagining only the most adverse outcomes; we believe that we have a crystal ball - one which is quite black, of course - and we convince ourselves that what we "see" is what will happen for sure. In addition, our mind does not focus on seeking solutions, but rather assumes that there are none. In this scenario, concern and worry no longer serves its purpose to prepare us - it only causes anguish. Then, if the worst does happen, having gone around and around about it in our head means that when we do have to face the situation, we are full of anxiety and totally unable to react. Our preconceived notion that we won't be able to face it has also given rise to a sense of helplessness (learned many times in our past). Worry thus ceases to help us and becomes so intense that it becomes a problem. In addition, we often get overwhelmed thinking about things that will never happen, which leads to unnecessary suffering. Once the situation is over, we won't be aware the next time we look into our crystal ball and see a dark future, that we failed in our predictions and would never be able to make a living as a fortune teller. We stay convinced that the worst will happen and, as we will see later, intense convictions tend to be erroneous precisely because of that conviction.

Healthy concern is called common sense, and we actually need it. If we think that everything is going to go well, we won't have a contingency plan ready, and we'll have to improvise on the fly. Moreover, if we don't have healthy concern, it can greatly diminish our capacity to react. A certain degree of concern helps us prepare solutions, and it is a valuable resource.

Each emotion has, as we have seen, a sound function, but perhaps we don't see it as so. The rejection of any of them upsets our emotional regulation, because the process of regulation of our emotions has much to do with how we react to them[10]. We can't decide what we feel - although we sometimes want to do so - but we can change what we do with our emotions when they occur. Let's take a look at these issues in more detail:

1. **Emotions are our sensors to understanding the world and ourselves.** By paying attention to them, we can make better decisions. To do this, we must learn to connect with our emotions and feelings, rely on them, and let them be. We must regain the capacity to listen to ourselves.

   An exercise for doing this is to set a stopwatch for one minute, and during that minute, just watch our emotional state and our feelings. Even if we live on an emotional roller coaster, most of the time we don't ever stop to observe ourselves carefully. At the beginning, those 60 seconds can seem like an eternity to us. What also might happen is that we won't notice anything, and in that case, looking at our body can be helpful, noticing how fast and deep our breathing is, which area is tenser, and which is more relaxed, where there is more heat and where it is colder, our posture, etc. Initially, it is best to do this in times of relative calm, where our feelings are more manageable. Over time we may also do so when our discomfort is more intense.

2. **Emotions tell us what we need and how to get it.** They are not simply a passive process of perceiving what things mean for us; they also involve *an action.* Rage drives us to fight, sadness to seek comfort, and guilt to improve our performance. If we find ourselves in a blocked emotional state, but we do not move in search of what we need, it's possible for that emotion to get stuck inside, telling us loudly that there are unmet needs, while we try to numb, avoid or bury them. It is important for us to at least realize what our emotions ask of us and what it is that would help us to provide this. If we are unaware of all these issues, there may be curious paradoxes, for example, we may feel profound loneliness but, instead of seeking company - which would meet the underlying need linked to that emotion - we tend to isolate ourselves from others, making our loneliness even more intense.
3. **Emotions tend to flow.** We can hold them back temporarily, but not permanently. Emotional control is literally bread for today and hunger for tomorrow. Many people who feel incapable of dealing with their emotions spend a great deal of energy trying to keep them under control. This system will collapse sooner or later, for example when something happens that exceeds our ability to contain it, when various circumstances come together, or they are accumulated one after another over the years. Control as a psychological mechanism is problematic in that when things happen that are beyond our control - and in life these kinds of situations are unavoidable - if this is our only system, we are left without any alternative. It takes time to regain a level of emotional functioning in which we can let our emotions flow, modulate them and regulate them, but it is very important.
4. **Emotions are intertwined.** When we reject our emotions or try to control them, we can block this process. Sometimes, we may notice an emotion very clearly, and then switch to another emotion, for example, moving from pitying someone to hating them, from being sad to becoming enraged. If we let them free, emotions run like colors do for a painter. When they are put on a canvas, they are combined to form a landscape. This landscape will represent our

internal emotional state when we face a certain situation; it will tell us what it means to us. We can handle the brush, but not decide which colors will be in the painting, because that depends on the colors of the real situation (the day is bright, the night is dark) and the palette that we have. When emotions are mixed, we operate better. For example, we can get angry (rage) with someone who we love (affection), then while we explain to the person what is bothering us, we don't forget that we are talking with someone whom we appreciate, so we choose nice words to keep from hurting them. Or we can feel sadness and at the same time lean on someone close to us. There is no better cure for sadness than a hug, as affection may help dilute the pain. Many people who have suffered from interpersonal trauma have enormous difficulties with these combinations of emotional states. They may never get angry with the people they love and allow negative situations to go on for too long, which greatly complicates relationships. Quite often sharing their sorrow, asking for help and receiving comfort are also difficult for them. They assume that all relationships will be the same as those that damaged them in the past and as such deprive themselves of important resources for regulating their emotions.

5. **The important thing is not what we feel, but what we tell ourselves about it, and what we do with it.** What we say to ourselves modulates the intensity and adjusts the emotional response, as if we were managing radio controls. Our internal thought process can operate like an echo chamber that strongly increases emotional intensity, or it can attenuate the effects of emotions, making them more manageable. For example, a phrase that usually causes emotions to rise is when we say to ourselves, "I can't stand feeling like this." Let's try with any emotion that we notice at the moment and while observing it, repeat to ourselves, "I can't stand it" over and over. We will see how the sensation increases and becomes unbearable. It's as if we tried to go up 50 rungs of a ladder, saying to ourselves the whole time, "I'm tired, I can't do it, this ladder is so high, I'll never make it to the top." Climbing the ladder will become torture. If we do something different, turn our mind to what we want to reach up top and distract our attention from the difficulty of the climb, we are still tired but everything is much more bearable and we don't suffer. Becoming aware of our internal dialogue and making changes to it

is a very powerful emotional regulation tool.

6. **We should give ourselves permission to feel.** We sometimes censor our emotional responses for different reasons. If we grew up with a person with a bad temper, we can try to be different, and never let ourselves feel or express rage. This leads to two possible problems. On one hand, we can accumulate rage until it eventually explodes. Not having learned to handle it, our rage will get out of control, and thus there is a greater likelihood of reproducing the model that we rejected the most. On the other hand, we can internalize rage, turning it against ourselves, telling ourselves the same things which that person said to us. As all the emotions make sense and appear when something triggers them, the only real alternative is to allow ourselves to experience them, to make them ours, to feel and express them in our way, not according to old models that we don't approve of.

   This does not occur only with rage, of course. We can't give ourselves permission to feel sad because when we move forward after hard times, we may think that if we get sad, we will be weak and lose that inner strength that kept us standing. We may also think that being weak is dangerous, because if when we were very little and vulnerable other people hurt us, our mind may equate being weak with being hurt again. Many people who have suffered in a relationship do not allow themselves to feel affection so as not to suffer again or do not get excited so as to avoid disappointment. If I try to decide by royal decree what I can and can't feel, it won't work. Our nervous system has been designed in a certain way, and we can't impose a different kind of functioning on it; we must play by its rules. If we try to control our emotions that way, our body will rebel against our "emotional dictatorship."

7. **Emotions do not compete or fight with each other.** When this happens, the emotional processing system becomes blocked. We said before that emotions are intertwined, but this does not mean that they should contradict one another. We feel conflicting things, because the world is contradictory, and that emotional mix helps us realize the nuances of the situation. The problem comes when, for example, we feel anger at being sad. Rage will block the sadness and won't allow it to flow, and then it may not leave. It doesn't matter how much we cry, it won't be cathartic, and we will feel suffering rather than relief. Another example is being scared of feeling sad,

because in the past we were very depressed and now we are afraid to find ourselves in the same state, or because we grew up with a depressed person, and our sadness connects us to those memories. In any case, fear will block the processing of sadness, and sorrow will remain inside us. Whenever it raises its head, we close the door or pay attention to another issue. The feelings that do not go out through the door, which do not reach the consciousness, which we don't let loose, will live inside us forever. Thus, the past continues to control our decisions in the present and paradoxically, leads us to keep repeating the issues from our past that we like the least.

4 MEMORIES IN THE MIST

If we don't know our own history, we will simply have to endure all the same mistakes, sacrifices, and absurdities all over again. Aleksandr Solzhenitsyn.

A situation can be experienced in different emotional states, with greater or lesser intensity. Once we leave the situation behind us, those emotions go away and make space for others that correspond to the new times. Many of these feelings do not leave a mark because the brain deems them irrelevant and discards them, while others will be stored in our memory archive. This is how we build a catalogue of significant experiences, which form the basis for our further performance. This catalogue is where we go to look for references of what to do when facing a new situation. Regardless of whether our experiences have been positive or negative, the collection of all of them constitutes our learning.

Some situations go beyond the ordinary experience because they are more intense, happen when we are more vulnerable, have significant people involved or are especially meaningful to us. Life-threatening events or experiences affecting our physical well-being or identity, or things that shatter our beliefs about ourselves, others and the world, can exceed the capacity of the nervous system to process them. Perhaps the situation ends, and sooner or later we feel better, but that memory has not been filed properly. It still needs to be to fully assimilated.

Depending on the type of problem we are going through and what it means for us, the blocking of emotions may become more powerful if the situation gets worse. If our way of regulating emotions is not finely-tuned, it can influence how emotional processing occurs, and how the memories are stored. For example, if we tend to avoid certain emotions and they are triggered during the experience, we will tend to deal with them through avoidance. If we usually suppress and drown our feelings when they become particularly intense and intolerable, we will do it even more. These memories and the related feelings that we avoid or try to suppress do not disappear, but they can't be passed on to the memory archive either. They remain there, in a particular state, conserving part of the initial thoughts, emotions and feelings.

The tendency to avoid or suppress emotions can continue to operate with those memories long after the situation has ended. Trying not to think about it or burying it allows us to continue to function in daily life. We push what happened out of our mind and focus on what we are doing. But when the situation is repeated or something triggers those feelings, the emotions and sensations that are related to them resurface and interfere with what we are doing. When this happens, if we follow our usual regulatory mechanism, we move them aside or push them down. These emotional regulatory systems - avoidance and suppression - are not completely effective and facilitate the development of various psychological problems.

In extreme and unbearable situations, when we are overwhelmed by what is happening, our nervous system may collapse. The emotional experience exceeds the capacity of our brain to process it, similar to when an electrical surge blows a fuse. This can manifest itself in many ways. It may be that we see what happens as if we were detached from ourselves, as if it were happening to someone else or even seeing ourselves physically from outside the body. It's possible for the physical or emotional pain to suddenly disappear. We may notice ourselves feeling numb, dizzy, or exhausted, or we may even faint. The full awareness of what is happening can turn into a feeling of going on auto-pilot. We can notice ourselves feeling emotionally blocked, paralyzed or disoriented.

The way in which an experience is assimilated also depends on how other people participate in it. The younger we are, the more essential the presence of others to regulate us is, but even as adults, we need to feel that support in very serious circumstances. Others can greatly contribute to our recovery from an event, not only at that particular moment, but when they give us their support afterwards or when we tell them what happened and share our emotions with them.However, others can also make things much worse and cause us to feel unbearable sensations Remember that what is most traumatic for human beings is the damage that comes from another member of our species. When someone we trust is the source of danger, the impact will be the greatest. And if it happens in childhood, when we are absolutely dependent on these people, the impact is far greater.

Experiencing something repeatedly is another factor that influences how much something affects us. For example, if we lost someone who was important to us during childhood, the loss of someone dear to us during adulthood may affect us more profoundly than it would have if we hadn't experienced loss in the first stage of our lives. If adverse situations occur frequently, the effect can be cumulative and sensitize us to whatever comes next. These memories that connect do not need to be identical, but they should share some common element and generate similar feelings. Our brain goes back to the archive to find references for the new situation, and if the clearest connection is a blocked memory, there is a strong likelihood that we will get blocked again now.

Whenever experiences occur that our system can't assimilate, the feelings that we experience in these situations do not disappear with the passing of time. Unlike memories that are processed and integrated completely, there are elements of unprocessed memories that remain active. We can try to push them aside or not think about them, but they are there. If we have experienced disconnection, emotional blockage, partial or complete loss of consciousness, paralysis or detachment from the situation, we can feel similar things when we remember them. Our system learns to associate the situation with the response from our brain, and when we try to evoke it later, or something reminds us of it, it will be activated again. If the situation has been prolonged or has been repeated many times, the conditioning of the reaction becomes stronger.

These memory blockages or feelings of disconnection may occur, not only when we try to think about past experiences, but also when something activates them in our daily life. We can notice memory gaps, that pieces of what we do become erased, that we have the experience of watching ourselves from outside our body, feeling emotionally disconnected or weird, or we experience our surroundings as foreign and unfamiliar. Something in the situation, which we are unaware of, has inadvertently connected with our old experiences, and the automatic response to them is activated. But our disconnection does not allow us to see those relationships between present symptoms and situations, and the past events, so we don't understand what is happening to us.

Sometimes things are subtler. We don't notice those feelings but still react to day-to-day things in a way that we don't understand. Our responses are disproportionate or do not fit; they do not seem to make sense. For example, if we got into a fender bender on the way to work, and then we jump out of our chair when someone slams a door, it makes sense. We understand that we are still nervous due to the accident, the fear is still in our body, and the alert level has not yet dropped. However, this type of sensation can last years or reappear much later, and in that case, it would be more difficult to connect the element that triggered the current reaction with the initial memory that was blocked.

If the emotional blockage is intense, and conditions to resolve it do not exist, access to these memories can be permanently disrupted. It's possible that we won't realize all this, that we will review the situation and not notice anything. We believe that we are over it, that it does not affect us. The sooner something happens, the longer the situation lasted for, and the closer we are to the people involved, the more likely it is that we will face higher levels of blockage. With time fog may cover it all. If we look back on our childhood or a particular time, the memories seem blurred. We can see everything as detached chroniclers who know what happened, but who apparently do not feel anything. Perhaps we might notice a refusal to look closer, as if stopping to think about those stages were a dense, laborious or irritating task. If we don't remember anything or our memories are incomplete or inaccessible, our keys to understanding ourselves or our position in the world won't fit. Therefore, we will make blind decisions or, at the very least, decisions we have little understanding of.

Old and unprocessed experiences not only continue to influence but also interfere - in a very powerful way - with how we live in the present. The lower our awareness of what happened is and the greater its importance, the bigger its impact. We may notice a centrifugal force that separates us from those memories, but at the same time, there is a strange attraction. We say that the past is over, that dwelling on it is of no use, that we don't care about it or that we have to leave it behind. But it still has a powerful hold over the way we live now. The more we try to push it aside, the more the feelings, emotional blockages or our own memories will assail us unexpectedly. If the fog is dense, we won't have any idea about the origin of the issues that come to our mind. Or if we do, we might say, "This can't have happened, I'm imagining it" or we simply push it away again and again because we don't want to think about it.

The attraction that these unresolved memories produce is proportional to our phobia to go back to them. We are trapped in an endless loop. The more we try to go forward, the more everything seems to come back. It's as if we are still tied to them by a rubber band that pulls us further back the more we advance. Sometimes we get to keep them buried until our life circumstances connect with them, and then everything emerges as if we were repeating the initial situation. These vital circumstances that trigger our blocked memories are recollections that sometimes defy logic; they are completely unrelated but generate identical feelings of helplessness, and powerlessness, etc. Since these circumstances are apparently so different from one another, we don't see how they are related. On other occasions, the old patterns can be triggered by a relationship that activates a previous attachment issue, or if our children reach the same age that we were when something happened to us.

People who grow up in dysfunctional families may try to make a life for themselves away from the original context, sometimes moving to another city or country. For many years, everything may seem to go well; they can hold down a job or form another family but, quite often, a paradoxical situation can occur. Seemingly by chance, their circumstances may change; they lose their job, or their family breaks up, and there doesn't seem to be any other choice but to return to their original home where they grew up, to that place that they hoped they'd never go back to.

Although this may not happen, the thread that unites us to our unresolved past is not broken simply because we don't think about it. We only pretend that it isn't there. Sometimes our mind achieves this in such an efficient way that we don't remember anything at all, or we erase certain episodes to the point of not having any idea what happened. But one day, that past will catch up with us. The memories

- which want to be filed with others - slip into our thoughts, feelings or dreams, because the way that they are stored is unstable.

This reactivation of our past does not only occur when related things happen, but also precisely when everything seems to be going well. It can happen when there is no apparently logical reason for this to come about; but if we think about it, it makes perfect sense. When we are facing a difficult situation, we can't stop ourselves to examine how we are feeling, at least not all the time. Our attention and our mental resources must focus on overcoming the problem. If the circumstances are persistent, the system must work this way for a long time. When the situation ends, the natural outcome - if we don't become blocked - is to depart from those patterns and start performing differently. We can decrease the alert level, relax, and then realize - usually better than when we were immersed in the circumstances - how much anguish we experienced or how tired we are. It's possible that our system won't know how to return to non-defensive functioning if we have lived in an adverse context for a long period of time. But sometimes it maintains the ability to detect that the situation has passed. Then, when we are at our best moment in life, the memories can coming flooding back for no apparent reason, and we think, "Why am I thinking about all of this again?" We feel bad precisely when everything is going better and wonder, "Why now?" The reason why this happens is that our body is wise and understands that we can now allow ourselves to become aware of our wounds, and to stop and take care of them. The mist is no longer necessary and begins to dissipate.

At this time, if we understand what is happening and dedicate some time to looking back and understanding our history, many things may fall into place. It's important to look at ourselves without judging or reproaching anything, seek out the necessary support, and focus on understanding ourselves in a deeper, more complete way.

When memories do not come spontaneously, and we only have memory lapses, disconnections or symptoms in everyday life, it's equally important to stop ourselves and figure out what is happening. We often ask ourselves, "Why is this happening to me?" but underneath this question there is no real attempt to understand. We are simply blaming ourselves for having the problem and pressuring ourselves to escape. The real key to better understanding our own selves is to detect what triggers our disturbance. The relevant question is: what happened just before we started to feel strange, disconnected or bad? Let's not seek dramatic events, problems or conflicts. Triggers can be seemingly insignificant; it's only when we have all the pieces of the puzzle that they will make sense. For example, we can see that we were disconnected when we woke up in the morning, after having had an unpleasant dream the meaning of which we did not understand. Perhaps it happens when we see certain movies that we like, but that also disturb us. It may not be something that happens, but something that doesn't happen when we expect it to - if our partner doesn't call us, or our mother doesn't care to find out how we're doing. These are normal circumstances, sometimes predictable things, that we don't think should affect us, but they do. Identifying these triggers, both external and internal, is a way to get to understand what happens to us.

This is not to say that we should try to become detectives of our own history. We must not explore the fog of our brains and try to force our memories out. We can be sure that if our mind does not let those memories come out, it's because it knows better than us and that we are not yet prepared to assimilate everything that they contain. It's not that an adult can't face any experience that they have had, no matter how hard it is. Human history makes this clear with all the terrible things that people have had to face throughout history. But let's think that if we are disconnected for a long time, we can't be aware of what it means to recover those memories. Doing so is crucial but delicate, and it should be done through a careful, gradual process.

Remembering the blurred areas or having a memory that works well now is indeed a goal, but it should not be the first one. It's essential to be able to function in a more appropriate manner, to have a better sense of well-being and to learn to relate. It's true that, coming from a complex history, only by becoming conscious of our past can we modify our present problems. But it's also true that diving head first into traumatic situations may generate unproductive suffering. It would be as if we were reliving them without being able to solve anything. There are many aspects that we need to approach first, such as the way in which we take care of ourselves, regulate our emotional states, and understand our reactions. Changing the patterns of behavior that cause us problems will make us feel more stable and more sure of ourselves.

Generally, many memories come to us spontaneously as we go through this changing process. When this happens, progression is more natural, and we have the time to match the pieces and understand their meaning. Not until we have assimilated a part of our history does it make sense to go on to another part. If everything comes at the appropriate time, it will keep us from getting overwhelmed. The emotions and sensations associated with those memories may have a similar intensity to the moment that they were generated and be more vivid than we initially thought. Those memories were contained, encapsulated or isolated for a long time and it's better to access them gradually.

Moreover, before touching on our memories, we should have information that helps us understand them. We need to understand many things about how our mind, emotions and relationships work. It's important to realize which difficulties we actually have and adopt a realistic perspective on how to change them. On one hand, it's essential to learn to accept ourselves as we are. On the other hand, we must be willing to make a profound change in our patterns of functioning, especially in the way that we take care of ourselves and how we relate to other people. Many things must be established to keep us from getting overwhelmed when we face our more difficult memories; this way we can assimilate everything they bring with them. Then the work of reviewing our history becomes much simpler and more fluid.

We might think that having made all these changes, opening old wounds won't be necessary; but if we want a stable and solid improvement, it's important that we're able to face every stage of our life with complete normality. When we do it, any experience, no matter how hard it was at the time, will no longer determine who we are now and what the rest of our lives will be like.

The question is not whether it's worthwhile or not to look back, but how to find the appropriate time and pace to do it properly. We have to find a balance between avoiding dwelling on the past out of fear of suffering and forcing ourselves to do things we are not yet ready to do. By doing things this way, we learn something very valuable: to take care of and respect ourselves.

5 THE SURNAMES OF DISCOMFORT

You cannot untie a knot if you do not know how it is done. Aristotle.

Often, we feel bad, but we don't understand what is happening to us, how it started or why it is happening. We are flooded with discomfort and don't know how to escape it. Our emotions are unnamed or mixed up with one another. We have constant mood swings, which make us feel as if we were on an emotional rollercoaster, with no ability to control when we go up or down, or how fast everything goes. Our state of mind is like an unpleasant, variable climate, to which we are exposed. Sometimes we don't understand the connection between our changing mood and the circumstances that surround us. What triggers our discomfort? How does it start? What circumstances feed it and keep it alive? What sensations do I end up feeling?

The emotions, as we have seen, are our sensors, but for them to work, we must stop and listen to them. However, more often than not, we don't stop to reflectively observe what happens to us. We repeat over and over that we feel bad and tell ourselves that we shouldn't feel this way, that there are no problems that justify this mental state. But by doing this, we don't feel better and still don't understand anything; we only heighten our anguish and get angry with ourselves for feeling bad. Maybe we ask ourselves why we feel this way. But we don't do it out of a real curiosity to understand, but instead just to reprimand ourselves for having a problem. We can be so upset by our inner feelings that we don't want to stop to notice or understand them. We try to control what we feel and think or even do things that prevent us from perceiving them, like taking medication, busying ourselves with endless activities, seeking out intense emotions that separate us from unpleasant sensations or even hurting ourselves or thinking about doing so, all to avoid looking inward and being aware of what we feel. But, as we said in the introduction, what is not understood cannot be changed.

Something essential to increasing the understanding of our experiences is to identify what its components and nuances are. Just by observing different aspects of a problem does not make change happen by itself, but it is essential to finding really effective solutions. Discomfort does not appear without a reason. There are, as we said, triggers that activate a first emotional state that may unconsciously resonate with previous unresolved experiences, giving rise to the emergence of the next one, like dominoes. Many times, we are only aware of how we feel at the end, when the avalanche has already occurred.

If we are very disconnected from our memories, if we aren't aware of what experiences have affected us and to what extent they still influence us, we will miss a key piece to understanding our reactions. Oddly enough, something similar can occur starting from the opposite situation. If we are constantly inundated by memories that overwhelm our minds, it will be as if we are seeing them from too close up to be able to gain perspective. It's not good for us to relive all our past experiences all at once - it's better to do it in a planned way, as we will see later. To understand the connection between the present and the past, we only need to realize how different experiences are linked. When something happens now, our brain will search our memory archive for previous experiences that can serve as a reference to know what to do. If those memories were not completely assimilated - whether we are aware of this or not - what we feel now is going to be multiplied by the resonance with all of the above, even if we are not consciously thinking about those situations. Thus, we may notice that our reactions are disproportionate to what is happening at the moment, but in fact, they are proportionate if we look at our history as a whole.

Not looking back denies us information about the origin of our current problems. Not looking inward prevents us from broadening our understanding of the problem. Emotional disconnection, that is, not wanting to feel our emotions or struggle with them, leaves us without major keys to understanding what is happening to us. This is not always a conscious phenomenon; sometimes we just know very little about emotions, simply because we grew up in a family in which these issues weren't discussed much, or over time, we have detached ourselves from what we feel, without doing so intentionally. We need to learn to identify the ingredients that make up the discomfort and the nuances of our feelings. It's important to stop and notice ourselves, to observe our emotions closely, without escaping from them and without judging ourselves for feeling this way. It's also essential to be able to look at our inner feelings without getting immersed in them, and see them with a certain distance and perspective. If we can't pin a name on our discomfort, identify the sequence in which these different elements are strung together, and reflect on it, we won't be able to stop the avalanche.

Once we identify the triggers and the sequences of the emotional states that give rise to our discomfort, we can make changes. The fact that these processes are automatic is one of the reasons they always get repeated in the same way. It's as if we were passive spectators of an atmospheric event, and we feel just as capable of modifying our emotional state as of changing the climate. Switching from automatic to manual allows us to take the controls. Even if we take time to learn how to drive, we can begin doing different things. When we want to change a repeating pattern that we don't like, doing something different - whether it works or not - is a step forward.

Another significant piece of information that we can draw from observing our activation sequences is that we can become aware of an intriguing fact. Our reaction to our initial feeling of discomfort, and the ones that follow, often end up worsening the first feeling. For example, if we had a childhood lacking in affection, it's common for us to have a deep feeling of loneliness inside. When a person doesn't call us or understand us, this can trigger a feeling of loneliness, which may activate rage against the world, making us say, "I'm better off alone." If we don't stop to carefully examine how we feel, we won't realize that by isolating ourselves we are just feeding our painful feeling of loneliness. By going in the room and closing the blinds, we fall into self-neglect, and end up doing to ourselves what was done to us. Our system tends to automatically gravitate towards known patterns, but we won't realize that this is happening if we tell ourselves that we don't want to go out or see anyone, without questioning our thoughts. As we will discuss later, an important aspect to solving this problem is not to take our beliefs as absolute truths and to learn how to make changes to the questions we ask ourselves. The relevant question is not whether we want to do something or not, but whether or not it is *good for us*. If we want to improve, learning to take care of ourselves must be a priority.

We describe below some of the emotional states[11] that can be activated. The exercise consists of choosing among the states that have the most to do with us. Some states may be more obvious than others, because our rejection of feeling certain things, or our tendency to disconnect ourselves from emotions, can make us believe that they don't produce any reaction. It's important therefore that we stop to notice and carefully observe if they generate any sensations for us. We can see if we start breathing faster or whether it becomes more difficult to breathe; if our stomach clenches or, if our body tenses up, or if there are any other difference in our physical state as we read certain descriptions. These feelings and beliefs may be familiar because we experience them constantly or because they are activated from time to time. In any case, all the emotional states that cause a reaction in us, however slight, should be considered. Below are a few examples, each with a brief description.

Abandonment

Inside of me there is a feeling of deep loneliness that never goes away. I feel that I have been left totally and absolutely alone in the world. Even when there are people around me, I am convinced that the important people in my life will not continue to be there because their feelings towards me might change, or that they won't stick around, or that they will die or leave me for someone else who is better. I believe that no one will remain in my life. Nobody will stay with me.

I am unlovable

I don't think that anyone can love me, or that I can capture anyone's interest. Nothing makes me worthy of the love from others; I am not special. No one cares for me or will ever be interested in me.

Everyone is going to abuse me

I am convinced that, if they have the chance, people will use me for their own selfish ends. I feel that I always end up being deceived or that I always get the short end of the stick. I am a victim.

I am a failure

I think that I will fail at anything I do, that I do everything in the wrong way, that I get everything backwards. I feel stupid, incapable, and untalented. I'm worth nothing, I'm incompetent, I'm a disappointment to everyone, and especially to myself. I'm never going to get anywhere.

I don't belong

I feel isolated from others, I feel that I am different, or that I don't fit in. I don't have a place in the world, I don't belong to anything or any one group. I can be surrounded by people and still have the same feeling, no matter how others behave.

My laziness controls me

I have no self-control or discipline, I get frustrated easily, and that gives me excuses to do nothing. I avoid exertion, complications or responsibility. When I feel tired, it's reason enough not to do anything. If I say to myself, "I don't feel like doing this," I believe that it's the only thing I have to keep in mind.

I need the approval of others

Getting other people's approval or recognition concerns me more than my own needs. I rely heavily on the opinions and reactions of others, and I'm very aware of the effect that my comments or my actions have on them. If I know that they disapprove of something, I am incapable of doing it.

I am incapable

I can't see myself being capable of adequately handling my day-to-day responsibilities without relying on the help of other people. I don't think that I can do things on my own. When I think "I can't," I experience it completely and literally, without questioning it; I don't even try. I ask others to take care of things, resolve my uncertainties or guide me, even when I already know what they are going to say.

Anything that can go wrong, will go wrong

I am pessimistic. My focus is on the negative side of life, and I overlook the good or optimistic things. Of all the possible outcomes, I convince myself that the worst will happen, and I see that negative future as certain and unavoidable. I don't consider alternative possibilities. My expectation is that things will go wrong or get worse.

I am wound up

I feel full of energy, as if I could deal with anything. I do much more than is reasonable, as if I were unaffected by fatigue. I have a thousand ideas and projects, and all seem possible and interesting to me. I'm euphoric, I can take on the world. I notice sometimes that I'm running myself into the ground, that I'm too hyperactive.

I am ashamed of myself

I feel flawed, defective, and inferior. I think that if others see how I really am, they won't like me. I can't show my inner self, I must hide what I feel.

I am fragile and vulnerable

I don't see myself being able to face life. I think that everything will affect me, that I won't be able to withstand a hit. I am small and weak. I view my vulnerability negatively, as if anyone could destroy me effortlessly, as if any disease could kill me.

I'm helpless and unprotected

I have no barriers and no defenses for whatever comes at me. If someone wants to harm me, there's nothing I can do to prevent it. I'm exposed to danger, I have no way of defending myself, and no one will do anything to protect me.

I'm trapped

I can't go anywhere; I'm stuck in situations, like a fly trapped in a spider's web. This feeling is so intense that I can't see any alternatives or ways out. I feel locked in or even paralyzed. I can see the options, but I am unable to choose one.

I'm confused

I don't know what I feel or think. I easily doubt myself. My opinions, as well as my emotions, change from one moment to the next. A lot of the time, I can't even think, I'm really out of it, and unaware of what is happening around me. Sometimes my head is a mess, and I don't know which way to go.

Without others, I am nothing

I can't be happy without other people. If they leave me, I feel like I'm in a dark hole, as if I had disintegrated completely. I don't feel complete, I feel empty without another person. It's as if I can't exist unless someone else is with me; the loneliness is unbearable and agonizing. I desperately cling to people, because when they distance themselves, I feel like I'm dying.

I feel rejected

My perception is that everyone rejects me, that no one likes me. I feel that there is something about me that makes it so that no one will accept me. I'm very sensitive to any gesture of contempt or to being sidelined. I focus on people's glances, comments, and attitudes, to identify any signs that they might turn on me.

All these states can alternate in a matter of seconds and activate sequences that often recur. If we don't pay attention to each one of them, we might only notice the last state we experienced. Other times we see part of the sequence, but we feel powerless against their unleashing, as if we were observing a storm that can't be stopped. If we become aware of these processes, identify what triggers them, and figure out what the first thing that fires is, we can move from this automatic state to a more reflective one, and this can become a starting point for change.

For example, I feel bad, I go out and start drinking until I get blind drunk. Then I feel very guilty and terrible for having done this. But, where did everything begin? We can't even remember. So, we think back and reflect, "Let's see, two days ago things were going quite well, I haven't had a downturn like this for a long time. But then there was that night when I didn't sleep a wink - what happened that day? Nothing out of the ordinary, really. Well, yes, in fact, that argument with my partner, but just like all the other times." We stop here a bit to take this point in, asking ourselves what sensation remained after that discussion, and what is the first thing that comes to our mind when we think about this? We always take a minute, stop to think, and let the memories come. This way we can remember the face of our partner when she said, "You're just like your father." If our father was an alcoholic who made our mother suffer all her life, that comment makes us feel like we have been accused of the worst possible crime, which is the last thing we want to feel . The memories of our childhood experiences are painfully activated, and for a moment we feel fragile and vulnerable. Our partner's rejection of us also triggers the need for approval. It started growing inside us when we were children and attempted unsuccessfully to obtain recognition and affection - as all children do - from a father who humiliated and despised us. These emotions trigger protective responses of intense anger and fear; our system wants to fight against the pain that we feel and to escape from both the present situation and the connected memories from our past. But we don't allow ourselves to be aware of our rage, because we identify this emotion with the hostile father we had, and we don't want to be like him. Our fear is also blocked, ever since the times we heard screaming and fighting at home from which we could not escape. We feel trapped, just like those times in childhood, even though we are now adults with more options. The trigger is the look on our partner's face, and the sequence is a feeling of fragility, the need to please, then rage and fear, and finally, blockage. We may turn to alcohol to numb the initial feeling, stop the sequence, self-punish for provoking the other's rejection or because when we get enraged, we re-enact our father's typical reactions. Drinking generates very ambiguous feelings because there is a certain decrease in sensations when the alcohol takes effect in our system; we no longer notice anything. But after the alcohol wears off, we feel physical discomfort due to the hangover, the sleepless night, and the infinite guilt because of having done exactly - but not by chance - the same thing that our father did. Automatic sequences paradoxically lead us to the last place that we would like to go.

If we observe the way one emotional state leads to another, we can stop judging ourselves and understand that automatizing is to blame. Torturing ourselves over a problem is not going to change anything, but we can gain perspective and change the situation by working it out. To achieve this, we must make changes in the sequence. Since we are now adults, we can afford to leave situations, for example, to stop having a discussion before it becomes too intense. Another option is to have a conversation with our partner to explain to them how we feel when we hear these things. If they are aware that what they say is harming us, we'll try to understand what they are protecting themselves from, and whether it has to do with us or with their own stories. We must be honest here. We can "inmunize" ourselves against our need to please others by saying what we think more often; we can also prevent ourselves from feeling fragile, protect ourselves from what might harm us, and stop others who want to harm us or avoid doing things that might harm us. Another possibility is to imagine taking care of a vulnerable child and understanding why this child felt the constant need to please others.

Merely stopping to observe what is activated within ourselves, and what it connects with, trains us and improves our ability to reflect on what is happing to us. If we do it often enough, we'll notice that we are slowly shifting from automatic to manual. This capacity to observe oneself, to get perspective and to see the changes in our mental state with certain distance, and with the intention of understanding without judging, is in itself, a powerful tool for regulating our emotions. If we work on this consistently, the effects can be significant in the medium term.

The sequences can be very different, even with the same person. Different triggers can activate one emotional state or another, but usually there will be some that occur more frequently or that are problematic; these are the ones that we would like to work on first. We shouldn't worry about finding the single key for change; the important thing is to stop and understand our reactions in detail and see how they are linked. Once the sequence is identified, any variation which is introduced will be useful, regardless of the outcome. As long as what we do is not more of the same, we have already stopped our automatic behavior. If we modify one of the steps of the choreography, the next step won't be the same. We won't notice major changes until more time passes, but we have to take responsibility for working on it if we want to improve things. Pretending that it didn't happen or that it wasn't important, or regretting it later or getting angry with ourselves, won't prevent this from happening.

6 LISTENING TO THE BODY

Several sorts of memory exist in us; body and mind each possesses one peculiar to itself. Honoré de Balzac.

Conventional wisdom has always been ahead of neuroscience. A popular saying is that our heart hurts when we are suffering because of someone, or we say that we have "gut feelings." For many years studies on the nervous system have focused on the brain, in the same way that psychology gave primacy to thoughts or cognition compared to other elements. These theories pointed to our ideas as the things that generated our emotions. Despite the fact that our perspective on things can influence how we feel about them, this is only a very small part of the processes that lead us to regulate our internal states and operate in the external world.

Stephen Porges[12] has defended the idea of the importance of the peripheral nervous system in the regulation of emotions. It is the fluid interaction between body and brain from which a good modulation of our emotional states and an adaptive response to the environment that surrounds us emerge. In this system, peripheral nerves would cover two main areas: the heart and the viscera, the chest and the abdomen. In fact, the relevance of the nervous structures associated with the digestive system have gained more importance in recent research, and some of their complex functions are starting to be understood.

The digestive system has more nerve endings than any other organ in the body. Many people notice how situations have an impact on their stomach and intestinal functioning. Similarly, it has been proposed that the digestive system, including the intestinal flora that populate it, could have an influence on our mental state. A very common disease, irritable bowel syndrome, seems related to this brain-body connection and its imbalances[13].

Another very important system is the heart, which also has a great number of nerve endings, and whose function seems to go beyond simply pumping of blood to the organs. In particular, the interrelated function between the heart and the breath is related to the regulation of the peripheral nervous system, and through it, to the brain. Even when we are at rest, our heart beats regularly, and its frequency varies with our breathing. If our heartbeat does not have this variability, our emotional and physical state will be worse. This is called heart rate variability or HRV[14] and we can train to improve it when it is out of synchrony. In fact, HRV training has proven to be useful in the treatment of many medical and psychological problems.

In the same way we pay attention to our emotional states, it is also important for us to listen to the information coming from our body. Just as an early or prolonged adverse history can lead to a struggle with our emotions or reactions, it can also generate different types of conflict with our body and its sensations. Absence of physical affection such as being touched lovingly or given hugs in childhood will later lead to a poor relationship with our body. As a result, we may view our body as a source of problems and irritation rather than associate it with pleasure or well-being. We pay more attention to unpleasant bodily sensations than to pleasant ones, and when we notice them, we don't know how to regulate them, or we do so in a way that will be counterproductive.

One of the possible consequences to derive from what was mentioned above is that we become disconnected from our body because we have never learned to feel it or because the signals that it sends us are so intense that they become intolerable. Once this connection is lost, the discomfort is still there, but we don't notice it - and therefore, we do nothing to change it - until it becomes a physical illness. By being disengaged from our body, we can detect pain or discomfort, but we don't understand the relationship between this pain and what is actually happening to us, nor do we connect it with what has happened to us in the past.

As described earlier, the basis for this brain-body relationship is established in our first years of life. When we are babies and we cry, we don't understand what is happening to us, and we are incapable of doing anything about it. We depend on an adult who is attuned to our discomfort and who is capable of figuring out what we need. So, our caregiver may say, "Time for bed, you're exhausted" or, "This child is starving, I'll give him a bottle." Of course, it is fundamental that, more often than not, the adult is correct in their prediction. When things work this way, we will gradually learn to detect what is happening to us and to find a solution that is aimed to satisfy our real needs. We also learn to delay that satisfaction when necessary, like not snacking in between meals or regulating and organizing our sleep schedule.

If adults don't understand themselves, they may not understand us either. If they function chaotically, our system will not have another model from which to learn how to self-organize. If our cues are misinterpreted, we may become confused about our feelings. For example, if whenever we cry, they give us the bottle so that we'll stop, we learn to turn to food in order to calm our anxiety. If another's response to our discomfort when we were children was to ignore it or minimize it, we won't have learned to name our feelings or their meaning, and we will also tend not to pay attention to them unless they become very intense and overwhelm us completely. If when we were feeling sick, adults told us that we shouldn't complain or scolded or ridiculed us for doing so, it is most likely that we won't be able tolerate a simple bout of the flu or allow ourselves to rest when we feel bad. If our caregivers were more afraid than we were when we fell ill, everything that has to do with diseases will be always experienced with great concern. If we were usually neglected except for the times we became physically ill, we will subconsciously tend to get sick when we need someone emotionally. Every time we find ourselves in a certain state, our brain will search its records for moments associated with similar past experiences, including how others around us reacted.

Sometimes, if the things that happened to us were related to our bodies, we can develop a specific rejection of everything that has to do with it. For example, if we suffered major burns, with the slow and painful process of recovery that this involves, we may have needed to disconnect ourselves from our body, and over time, we won't know how to regain that ability. Or if we had a problem or physical defect which led others to ridicule us, we may blame our body for being like it is. When our body has directly suffered attacks or abuses, connecting with it may lead us to connect with fear, disgust or shame, or bring back the memories of those situations that we are trying to avoid.

This rejection of the body can also be a manifestation of how little we like or value ourselves. When feelings of inferiority, of not being good enough, or of being unworthy or reprehensible develop, it is possible that we will avoid looking at ourselves in the mirror or that we won't like to see ourselves. This can happen either constantly or only at certain times, when we are in a particular emotional state or see a certain expression in the mirror that represents what we hate about ourselves or the personality trait we dislike the most. Sometimes this situation can be more extreme, and we don't even recognize ourselves. Upon seeing ourselves in the mirror, we say, "This isn't me," or "I don't recognize myself."

Another issue that we must keep in mind is that our body can become physically sick as a result of living through situations that have significant emotional impact, especially when they lead to a state of chronic stress. The effects of stress on the autonomic nervous system that innervates the body's organs and on the hormones that regulate different functions, as well as on the immune system that defends us from infections, have been studied extensively. Stressful situations can cause different diseases to develop, and influence their course. When we have physical problems and we are reluctant to focus on the resulting emotional aspects, or to reflect on our lives and relationships, we may seek medical treatments for those problems for years, which probably will be ineffective or have short-lived results. When drugs are not effective, and doctors suggest that the problem has a "psychological origin," many people tend to feel offended. We may feel that our discomfort or pain is very real, and "psychological" means that others think we are hypochondriacs. Unfortunately, doctors do not always adequately understand psychosomatic diseases, conversion disorders or somatoform symptoms, and all of these are problems where the psychological component plays an important role. It's not uncommon for professionals to say to their patients that they, "don't have anything," which - if we think about it - is quite insulting to someone who is feeling bad.

The physical problems that may result from traumatic experiences are very diverse. Some years ago, a study was conducted with thousands of participants in which the influence of adverse childhood experiences[15] were analyzed. Among people who had had four or more of these experiences, the chance of having cancer or heart disease more than doubled. The presence of physical symptoms that did not have any medical explanation also increased, and the greater the number of adverse experiences, the greater the number of symptoms. Individuals with a higher number of traumas smoked more, were more overweight and less physically active, and had more pulmonary and renal problems, more broken bones, and many other health issues. The paths that go from these adverse experiences to the development of different diseases vary widely, and are probably a combination of the direct influence of stress with poor self-care and fewer healthy habits. The way in which we take care of ourselves, as mentioned above, is primarily modeled on the way others took care of us during our childhood, and it will influence our physical care and the regulation of our emotions.

In any case, when we look at what is happening to us, and why it happens, we must take our emotions, beliefs, and physical sensations into account. We must understand both our psychological problems and our medical diseases. The treatment of any of these problems must cover both physical and mental aspects.

It's quite possible that we have never been able to have a good connection with our body or that we don't recognize its language. It's also possible that our body's sensations reflect feelings or emotions that we don't want to feel, because they remind us of moments that we want to forget or parts of ourselves that we wish weren't there. Perhaps we are consumed by debilitating physical ailments that cause us suffering, but are not aware of the relationship between this suffering and current or past adverse situations. The process of reconciling with ourselves must also include a reconnection with our body, and even more so in the circumstances described above. We need to relearn to feel, to look at our feelings and to learn how to describe them. Both positive and negative sensations vary depending on our emotions and thoughts. Even physical illnesses with a clear biological cause can be hastened, worsen or become more difficult to tolerate, depending on many life factors or internal psychological processes.

The first step is to calmly observe what we are noticing. Maybe our first thought is "I feel nothing," but let's examine this closely for a moment. What is our posture like, where are we distributing our weight, and how? Note the pressure of our feet on the ground. What part of our body is the warmest and what is the coldest? Where are we tense, and where are we relaxed? Where in our body is the heaviest and the lightest sensation? Describe in detail the most pleasant feeling. We should be aware of possible signals of discomfort and their detailed characteristics. Note all these sensations without labeling them, without concluding if they are good or bad or what they mean. Just let them loose, let them just be what they are.

Sometimes, by concentrating this way, we discover sensations that we were unaware of, and then we can better understand what we are feeling. Other times we observe that we were containing those feelings or making movements to distract ourselves from them, like clenching our fists or bouncing a leg up and down. Simply by becoming conscious of these details, and letting our sensations follow their own course, our discomfort often evolves further, and occasionally decreases or even disappears. Other times we may pay attention to the many thoughts in our head, and understand the effect that they have on our feelings. For example, if we constantly repeat, "I can't feel this, I want this sensation to go away" or think that if we stop noticing it, we will get overwhelmed, and we will observe that instead of subsiding, the discomfort increases.

This moment we connect with our body must be a continuously repeated experience for it to produce effects on our well-being and raise self-awareness. An exercise to help us with this is to learn to just sit and be with our feelings. When we notice discomfort, we locate it in an area of our body. Then we will place our hand on that area, without any pressure and without any effort to push the sensation away or pull it out, but with a gesture of care. We can imagine our feeling as a puppy, a kitten or a baby - whatever causes us to feel a sense of fondness - and that it is the pet or the baby who is feeling the sensation. We will then imagine ourselves mentally taking care of the animal or the baby, patiently transmitting the message that it is not alone and that it's going to get well. With the knowledge and acceptance that feelings are sometimes long-lasting, we simply sit with our emotions, without asking them to change or go away, without pressuring them or fretting over them, but just letting them be and remain as they are. Relaxation is not the aim of the exercise, but rather learning to tolerate our feelings and thinking of them with the attitude of a caregiver, instead of avoiding them or suppressing them emotionally.

In moments when we are calm and without any apparent

discomfort, we can try a version of this exercise by placing our hand over the heart, and learning to perceive its heartbeat and rhythm. We may also place our hand on our chest, and observe our breathing, how deep and fast it is. If it's shallow and fast, we can help ourselves to vary it consciously. We should be interested in breathing slowly, breathing out slower than breathing in. This change in how we breathe should be done easily and naturally; we shouldn't try too hard, and it shouldn't produce tension. We then place our hand on our belly, notice the sensations that come from it, and observe how it moves to the rhythm of breathing.

The sensations of discomfort can also help us understand our reactions to what is happening and our internal processes, of which we are unaware. Along with the emotional states described in the previous chapter, and the reactions of protection that will be discussed later, all these mental elements may arise sequentially, and automatically activate each other unless we increase our awareness of this. The more aware we are of what is happening to us, the greater our capacity to modify these sensations will be.

7 LEARNING TO REGULATE OUR EMOTIONS

Unexpressed emotions will never die. They are buried alive and will come forth later in uglier ways. Sigmund Freud.

Four girls are running and playing; they trip and fall down, skinning their knees.

Susana is five, and when she sees her knees bleeding, she goes home crying. Her mother affectionately says, "My poor darling, it hurts, doesn't it? Come here, let's clean you up. Yes, of course it hurts! I'll put a band-aid on it. Come and sit on my lap for a little while...." Soon the girl is feeling better, becomes bored and wants to go out and play. If the mother asks her if her knee still hurts, she will probably say 'no,' as she goes out the door.

Maria also goes home, and her mother is in the kitchen. She has been working all day and looks exhausted. Maria tells herself that her injury is not important and doesn't want to bother her mother with that. Her mother is so absorbed in what she is doing that she doesn't realize that something has happened to her daughter, and says, "Go wash your hands, it's dinner time."

Laura goes home in tears, and her mother runs to meet her. She has heard the girls' cries, and the first thing that comes to her mind is that something very serious has happened. When Laura's mother sees her, she grabs hold of her arms, screaming at her in anguish, saying "How many times do I have to tell you to be careful? You're going to give me a heart attack! We're going home!" Laura is very upset and still crying. Her mother says, "Stop crying, it's nothing... Come on, stop crying, you're going to make me sad."

Teresa goes for a walk before heading home, as the fall scared her and she can't stop crying. When she gets home, her mother says, "Stop crying or I'll give you a real reason to cry. You are always tripping, you are so clumsy, you've got to watch where you're going."

The type of care we receive is far more related to these small daily interactions than to extraordinary events. The way we understand ourselves and the world, what we do with our sensations, and our self-image, is shaped - so often in implicit or unconscious ways - by these day-to-day interactions[16]. The way in which we look at ourselves on the inside and our perspective on what we feel and think is modeled on how the most important figures in our childhood looked at us. These early relationships with our caregivers are a base template on which future interactions with significant people will be established. When these foundations are poorly constructed, the entire building ends up shaky. That is why it's necessary to start with a solid foundation. Many people try different treatments and therapies to solve their problems, but can't move on or change in the right direction. Sometimes the problem is that we begin building the house from the roof down. Our self-care pattern and the way we regulate our emotions should be established, at least partially, before we start working on other areas, so solid progress can be achieved.

But it's important for us to first understand the pathway from the small anecdotes of the four girls, to their further mental functioning.

Susana was lucky. In the lottery of "which type of family will I be born into" her prize was a mother with a secure attachment style. Let's take a look at the subtleties of their interaction. First, her mother acknowledges Susana's discomfort - she really notices how she feels. Perhaps that is the reason why Susana allows herself to cry naturally, and her mother can tolerate her crying. Second, her mother makes a gesture of care and busies herself by washing the physical injury and attending to her daughter's emotional suffering. From a child's perspective, Band-Aids are healing, along with the traditional phrases of "Let me kiss it where it hurts, if it doesn't feel better, I'll do it again." The interaction is playful, and it also introduces comfort when an adult says, "Come here, you poor thing, sit on my lap." The mother's cuddling lessens her daughter's pain and crying, until it disappears.

Aside from what Susana's mother does, it's also important to point out what she doesn't do. She doesn't scold her for falling, nor does she reproach her. She doesn't worry disproportionately, nor is she focused on her own emotions, but on how her daughter feels. She doesn't ignore the fact that her daughter is in pain or upset.

Thanks to all this, Susana has a model from which she can learn to be aware of how she feels, rate her emotions in a balanced way, pay attention to them, and regulate them. Her emotional regulation will be similar to the model described above. Her emotions will flow and mix, and she will develop resources to regulate or manage them. It doesn't matter if Susana has a more sensitive temperament, or if she is more easily frightened, embarrassed or impulsive than the average girl, because she will be capable of shaping these fundamental elements and function better as she matures. Although not everything depends on the environment, and we know we all have certain genetic predispositions, today it's clear that the environment has much to do with how these tendencies develop and shape our adult personality.

Now let's turn our attention to Maria's story. Notice that her problem is not that something bad happened to her, but rather that nothing has occurred that may help her learn good regulation. Her mother doesn't scold or punish her because she is simply too tired. And with regard to Maria, she did not come inside crying or seeking out her mother's attention, so this behavior seems indicative of a typical pattern. This style of attachment has been called dismissing. Having a bad day does not traumatize a child, but if we don't have the emotional energy to keep an eye out for his or her feelings, a great deal of opportunities for emotional learning may be missed. Maria will tend to tell herself that her emotional needs do not matter, act as if they do not exist, and not seek to satisfy them. She probably will learn to be self-reliant, to regulate her emotional states and not to turn to others for comfort or support. This deprives her of an important psychological resource, since we cannot do everything without help from others. At times, although we can do things by ourselves, it would be much easier and take less energy out of us if we leaned on someone. If we always make do without the support of others, sooner or later we will become overwhelmed and will be prone to developing psychological and physical symptoms. Since we don't have the keys to understand what we feel, when we notice these symptoms, they don't make sense to us and we don't realize where they come from.

What about Laura's case? Her mother is worried about her, which theoretically might seem good, but when this emotion is too great, it produces more problems than benefits. In families with preoccupied attachment, worry is considered synonymous with affection. Laura's mother thinks that the more she worries about her daughter, the more she loves her, and if she were to stop worrying, she would not be a good mother. At times, these messages are sent to Laura explicitly and transmit to her that she must always be worried and take control of the emotional well-being of others. Although these statements contain a partial truth, they are mostly a major distortion of the emotional bond.

Firstly, worry introduces density in relationships. It is like background music that creates a feeling of discomfort and makes situations more difficult. On one hand, we will try to get rid of that weight which becomes excessive but on the other hand, we will be trapped by familiar sayings and the moral obligation to worry about others and solve their problems. Bonds become ambivalent and the proximity may be asphyxiating. People who grow up in these situations often feel that they are trapped in an impossible dilemma. If we were to distance ourselves, we would be perceived as bad or selfish or that we don't love those who love us. If we stay, we will feel asphyxiated.

Secondly, constant worry on the part of our caregivers does not help us develop confidence in ourselves, and any activity causes fear, so exploring our possibilities becomes greatly limited. Just think the next time Laura goes to play with her friends. After the previous scene with her mother, she will be very careful not to fall again. She may be afraid of learning to ride a bike, climb trees or begin to do things alone. She will not only worry about hurting herself, but because the slightest damage can be emotionally experienced as if it were the end of the world, her sense of fear will be disproportionate to the situation. Furthermore, any minor accident will make Laura feel guilty for making her mother suffer. Children of preoccupied caregivers often tend to seek ways to calm them, because they are their source of safety, and their deregulation is extremely overwhelming for the child. As we can see, this image of a child calming an adult is an upside-down world. When Laura grows up, she may tend to be excessively in charge of other's discomfort, which does not really make sense, because adults can regulate themselves (or learn to do so). Trying to care for someone who won't care for themselves or trying to calm someone who won't calm down can only lead to frustration and despair.

These worried families do not foster children's autonomy. Worrying is a powerful glue, and separating ourselves is not easy. To adapt, children may absorb the way the system functions and become very dependent. They may feel very insecure when they do things by themselves and always seek out the adult to remain calm. This pattern can continue through adulthood and color all our future relationships. We won't be independent individuals or tolerate loneliness, distance or loss. We may feel others as parts of ourselves, and believe that we are nothing without them. Phrases like, "I am nothing without him," "I'd die without you," or "I'm empty without him," reflect this emotional dependence. No relationship works well if we can't imagine ourselves without the other person. From that sensation, every problem seems insurmountable.

Some individuals with this pattern can distance themselves, but not without a high emotional cost. Given the difficulties of working with those with whom they maintain a bond of preoccupation in the short term, they can choose to put some distance between them. However, there is an invisible thread that links them to these people, through which they receive guilt-inducing messages for not having called or gone to visit them or worried about how they are. Many times, to avoid this feeling of guilt, they yield to the requests of the other, for example, calling their mother whenever they get home, while at the same time they rant about having to check in with her even though they are now over 40. In relationships, they can become hypersensitive to any sign of others clinging to them, although internally they fight against their own dependence, which they are not aware of or reject feeling.

However, the most problematic outcome of this third pattern of attachment can come in a moment of interaction that appears to be positive at first glance. With the phrase "Come on, don't cry, it's nothing" the mother tries to help Laura to regulate her discomfort. However, it introduces the subliminal message that our discomfort is not important, and that we must get over it. Those sensations that we do not stop to notice can't be processed and will accumulate in our interior. Without this first step of emotional recognition, the rest of the regulatory process can't take place.

Finally, let's look at Teresa's case. She feels scared after falling down, probably because she anticipates what is about to happen at home. Teresa's mother has reactions that frighten her: where the girl should find solace, there is a source of threat. When fear is mixed with the bond with the caregiver, the system collapses because it is faced with a paradox[17]. The attachment system is a biological instinct aimed at protecting humans, because, as mentioned in previous chapters, the human species does not develop autonomously, but rather in the context of the family. The child, who lacks resources to protect itself from the environment, bonds strongly with a caregiver that performs that function. But this system is not designed for a caregiver that is both the source of security and the source of danger. Physical or emotional aggression cannot be assimilated. Even without that component, a frightened caregiver cannot be seen as a source of protection. Therefore, even if there are more people at home other than the most hostile or aggressive figure, if they can't protect us from harm, they can't function as secure attachment figures. The need to bond won't be satisfied, and protection will always be associated with that extremely complex connection. On one hand, we may feel abandoned, unlovable or unworthy, which reflects our unmet needs for affection. The feelings described in the previous chapters will arise and present different types of emotional deficiencies. These feelings will alternate with defensive reactions that are triggered when we connect with other people or with ourselves. Our mental processes will be dissociated, and our mind fragmented.

Now let's go to how these lessons are reflected in the way we take care of ourselves when we become older. Let's see if we can identify with some of these factors:

Are we self-destructive? Do we beat ourselves up mentally? Are we always self-critical? Do we do things even though we know they harm us? Do we get angry with ourselves for being wrong? Do we stop looking after ourselves physically? Do we ask for help when we need it? When help is offered to us, do we accept it? Are we looking for activities or positive relationships? Do we feel comfortable when others give us positive feedback? Do we realize what we need and see our own needs as important as the needs of others? Do we try to meet our needs? Is there a balance between taking care of others and ourselves? When we take care of others, deep inside - without recognizing it - do we hope that they will reciprocate or thank us for it?

All these aspects have to do with the way in which we take care of ourselves. If we see that we have problems with many of these issues, we can reflect on this: How can a person who treats themselves badly feel better? This is one of the cornerstones of the foundation that must be laid before anything else can be built: our efforts must focus on learning and on taking better care of ourselves, no matter the cost. The first step in solving a problem is to understand - without judging - how it has developed. How is the way I treat myself similar to the way my first caregivers treated me? Do I want to continue to function this way? Because *now that I am an adult*, I am the one who makes decisions. This does not mean that changing our self-care functioning is a simple process, but it is possible if we put our energy into it. By becoming aware of our internal processes, we are taking the first step.

8 IT'S NOT ME: A FRAGMENTED IDENTITY

One can't fight with oneself, for this battle has only one loser. Mario Vargas Llosa.

If we missed out on growing up under the gaze of another who sees who we are on a deeper level, the way we look at ourselves is going to be distorted from the beginning. There will be aspects of our personality that we can't accept, because they were ignored or repressed by the people who raised us. When we become adults, those aspects will operate outside of consciousness and we won't be able to regulate them. When these are activated, we don't identify with them, we don't understand why we feel, think or do these things. Our perception at that time may be: "It's not me, it has nothing to do with me, it has nothing to do with my character."

Our identity, the definition of who we feel we are, is learned in the mirror of our early relationships, and will be molded from interactions with significant figures throughout our life. When we express an emotion, if we see rejection in the face of the people we live with, we will internalize this rejection. If this experience is repeated when that emotion is activated, the rejection that we felt toward that emotional state will also be there. If this experience is repeated when that emotion is activated, the rejection we feel towards ourselves will also be repeated.

The parts of our personality that we don't identify with can be different[18], although it is frequent for this to happen with aspects related to vulnerability and rage. Here are some examples:

Why do we not like feeling weak or vulnerable?

"Sometimes I feel helpless, unprotected, that's the word. I don't know why I feel this way, because I am a very strong person. At work I face difficult situations, and I have no problem with it. But sometimes, in the most absurd manner, I feel so sad. I don't like feeling like that at all."

If we are children and our mother is depressed, we can't share our sadness. We tend to hide it, avoid it, bury or deny it. If our sadness doesn't receive recognition or consolation, it will be like a river whose course we dam with gates that don't ever open. At most, we may cry when no one can see us, but when we do it, our brain connects our state with our mother's sadness. It's a terrible thing for a child to see an important caregiver's sadness: a sad person can't be emotionally attuned to the child because they are overly focused on their own pain. It's this way because there is no harmony and resonance with the child's emotions, even if the mother fulfills her functions at the material level of caring for her child and believes they "don't lack anything." Sadness is an emotion that absorbs us and draws us into ourselves, generating a feeling of distance from others, something which is intolerable for a child who depends on these relationships in order to survive. If as children nobody taught us how to integrate, accept and regulate our sadness, we will try to avoid feeling it or will bury it deep within ourselves. But the emotions that we don't let ourselves feel, show or let out will remain inside us forever. The memories related to sadness will fall away, and then become disconnected and impossible to process. A part of us may feel infinitely sad, but we will contain it deep in our mind so that we don't notice it. This sad part will have no opportunity to evolve, to nourish itself with the rest of our experiences, and to interact with more emotionally supportive figures that we encounter throughout our lives. Deep inside us will always be the sad child that we refuse to be.

If the disconnection from this part of us is very strong, we may not be aware of this. Sometimes we only notice intense sadness and we don't understand where it comes from, and it will go hand in hand with the feeling of abandonment and loneliness that colored our childhood. We feel helpless, as if we were children with no one to comfort and care for us. We don't see ourselves as adults able to make changes, make decisions and find out what we need for ourselves - we feel small. We are still stuck in the "there and then." Only by rescuing this part of ourselves, reintegrating it, and learning to manage our sadness in other ways will we be able to let it flow and leave, and finally, actually live in the here and now.

The scenario that we have described is not the only one which may result in us not liking to feel weak or vulnerable. It's just an example, among many possibilities, of how those parts of us that we don't like have roots in our history. The important thing is that we realize what our own connections are if something similar to the examples mentioned above happens to us.

Why is it that we lose our tempers or don't like getting angry?

"I react in ways that aren't me - I don't recognize myself. I can be very hurtful, especially to people that I love. Then I feel very bad, but it works like a tightly wound coil, I can't keep it from happening or stop it. It's as if the anger controls me, and when it starts I'll even provoke others, just to make everything explode. This has nothing to do with me, in fact I hate violence because I have experienced a lot of violence."

Witnessing physical or verbal violence from significant figures, directed towards us or others, may modify our way of modulating rage. Rage, anger, and wrath, are emotions of the same spectrum, and they have to do with the instinctive fight response when we defend ourselves from external harm. If the attack comes from one of the primary caregivers or someone who represents an attachment figure (parents, partners and later our own children) our system will collapse when the responses of attachment and defense become simultaneously triggered. Both responses will alternate in close relationships. From this starting point it's not possible for our personality to develop in an integrated way. When the child is focused on the bond with the caregiver, he will put aside anger, because if he doesn't, he won't be able to form a bond. At that moment he will only see that he needs that person in order to survive and to feel safe. At other times he can feel the anger, and in that state, he won't have in mind that this figure is important for him on an affective level. There will be two contradictory responses to the caregiver: I need your protection and yet, I fear you. I need you and yet, I hate you. This duality will become our way of experiencing relationships with other people. We will feel a profound ambivalence to the idea of intimacy with others, and the closer we become, the more fear we will feel, and the more we will react against them or start to dislike them.

Disorganized bonds will be enormously complex and riddled with contradictions.. On one hand, the need for affection and protection was never met as the relationship, even in its best moments, was not healthy. A part of us remains fixed on this childlike need, which we identify with when we feel unable to live without our parents or partner and to function independently in daily life. We can also try to erase this part, reject it or disconnect from it to the point of not being aware that it's there. We will deny our emotional needs and tell ourselves that we don't need anyone. In any case, our needed inner child will remain inside us. Interestingly, what we have the least awareness of is what influences our decisions the most. For example, we can choose our partners from this very primary and childlike need for affection, and as adults, ignore all the signs that relationship is not going to work out. This situation explains why time and again we have relations with harmful figures, sometimes with curiously similar profiles, as if we can't learn from experience. Somehow, only our adult part is the one who learns from the experience. The child in need of affection that we don't want to see, isolated from the rest of our memories and our mind, has not been able to learn, has not been able to grow, and has not been able to evolve. If we let that child chose our partners, they will do so looking for the parameters that are familiar to them, looking for people who fit into the first mold related to affection and ties: the people we grew up with.

On the other hand, our rage may relate to other memory networks. From that perspective we will be aware of the damage and warning signs. This part of us can feel a deep hate and resentment towards the attachment figure. The rage will have a lot to do with our capacity to protect ourselves and those we care about, but we are uncomfortable with that rage, because something in our reaction reminds us of our aggressive attachment figure. We have most likely told ourselves, "I don't want be like this," because the last thing we want is to be like them. However, we cannot decide how our body reacts or what we feel. When it makes sense to feel rage, we feel it. And then this aspect of us will be activated, but we can't regulate it because we reject it, since we don't feel that it is part of us. We will try to push it inward and won't be able to access this energy to stand firm, say what we need or fight for what matters to us.

There is also another path that our mind can follow in the face of very contradictory and threatening caregivers. When we grow up in a world of extremes, where there are only victims and aggressors, our survival instinct can consider the side of the aggressor to be safer. We then reject being a victim, getting stuck in rage and resentment, in the fight against injustice or the belief of being strong above all. We never allow ourselves to be vulnerable, to connect to pain or feel compassion toward ourselves. We don't want to depend on anyone, because from that perspective, this is the only way to avoid being destroyed emotionally. We don't trust anyone, we don't establish bonds of intimacy, and we only relate to others in the form of domination, power or control.

Based on this scenario of early disorganized bonds, whichever side we identify with more, fragmentation in mental functioning will be extreme. The most rejected part - whether it is hostility or vulnerability - will be in the background, and we may be more or less aware of its existence. But these hidden parts, both our inner needy and helpless child and our defensive and protective rage, are going to play an essential role. When some mental processes come from any of these parts of us that we don't recognize, we are not identifying with our own feelings, thoughts or actions. We say to ourselves things like, "This isn't me," "Something is controlling me" or "I don't recognize myself." We will tell ourselves that we are not like this, but the truth is that we are the only ones who feel, think or act.

As mentioned before, the aspects of ourselves which we reject often have similarities with significant figures from our life. Therefore, our reaction towards that part of ourselves will also have to do with our initial reaction towards those figures in the past. For example, we can reject our vulnerable part because we feel a great resentment towards a mother who, mistreated by her husband, failed to protect us as children from our father's violence. Somehow, we don't differentiate our own pain, weakness or sadness from the person in whom we saw all these traits the most.We also cannot aceept our own rage and define ourselves as a quiet person who does not like conflicts and always tries to be in control, but from time to time we end up losing it and explode in an uncontrolled way. If this happens, our rage resembles the most frightening expression of that figure that marked our childhood too closely, and seeing ourselves acting like them can be painfully unforgivable.

These parts that we want to eliminate do not always manifest themselves externally. Rage can be internalized, and turn into ruthless self criticism or even a thought or an inner voice that does not seem to be our own. The level of rejection towards these parts, the degree of control that they eventually exert on the conduct or the complexity that they can achieve, is very diverse. Sometimes we can literally feel as if we were two different people, or we can't remember what happened while we were in another mental state. If the level of fragmentation of our personality is even greater, we can switch among many different emotions or reactions, be overwhelmed with wildly different, contradictory thoughts or not know what we actually think, feel or want.

Our life can become an unsolved puzzle. When our mind does not find a way to overcome these contradictions which feel unbearable, it may opt for one of two extreme situations. The first one is to live on an emotional roller coaster, in which intense and usually uncontrolled emotional reactions, all of which have very different natures, alternate with one another. In this case our beliefs may change so dramatically that we cannot define who we are. Our behavior is so contradictory from one moment to the next that it seems as if we are completely different people, depending on the situation. The second possibility, the other extreme, is to contain these reactions to such an extent that we don't even perceive them, and we impose on ourselves a constant and rigid control. These parts of our personality that we lock up can be silent, but consume most of our energy or get pushed outwards, manifesting themselves as impulses, thoughts, voices, emotions or feelings that we don't understand. We may relate these symptoms to a disease caused by external, genetic or unknown factors, but we don't connect them - in fact we are very reluctant to try - to any psychological factors, we don't see how they are linked to our life story.

9 OUR INNER VOICES: SPEAKING WITH OURSELVES

All your decisions are made by four or five people in your head, whose voices you can overlook if you are too proud to hear them, but they will be there next time if you care to listen. Eric Berne.

We all have an inner dialogue. We talk to ourselves about what is going on, what we feel and what we think. This internal discourse has a great deal to do with the regulation of our emotional states. The best decisions emerge from this dialogue between our rational and our emotional parts.

What we say to ourselves internally is gleaned, to a large extent from what certain people have said to us or what we said to ourselves with regard to what others did or didn't do. We take references from our significant relationships, starting with the people we who raised us, and continuing with all the other important figures in our lives.

Let's remember the girls with the scraped knees. Imagine them as adults, each having made a significant mistake.

Susana, who grew up in a secure attachment, will say to herself, "Way to screw up! I feel horrible, but well… I made that decision thinking that it was the best one. Now I have to deal with the consequences. I'll get over it. I've learned an important lesson."

Maria might say that it isn't a problem, that she doesn't care about the outcome. After this she will probably start suffering from increasingly intense headaches while she faces the negative consequences of her decision, but she won't link it to what has happened and will try to soothe her headache with painkillers.

Laura, the daughter of the worried mother, will become very distraught not only for what is going to happen, but also for many other negative things that could happen as a result, and also by how much she is going to make other people suffer.

Finally Teresa, beating herself up for having made that decision, will say to herself over and over that she is a mess, that she can't do anything well, and that everything is her fault. Of course, she won't tell any of her friends about this issue, and if she does so, she will neutralize the words of encouragement that her friends give her until they lose their effect. She won't know how to help herself or let others help her. This will cause many more problems and more discomfort than was initially generated. Moreover, Teresa will be less likely to learn from this mistake, because she won't tolerate the healthy guilt as well as Susana does, and she may end up repeating the same problem over and over again.

Here we can see that the internal dialogue model that each person uses is generated based on the external models they experienced when they made mistakes in the past. If these girls also experienced significantly traumatic situations, such as physical, emotional or sexual abuse, bullying, losses, and so on, things can become even more complicated. In Teresa's case, a child who grew up with disorganized bonds, the mental fragmentation that we described in the previous chapter will be greater because of the cumulative trauma. The level of internal conflict will grow exponentially, and the parts of her personality that focus on maintaining the link at all costs and which focus on defending against aggression will be even more irreconcilable. The level of rejection toward some aspects of her personality will be greater. Her angry part can get furious with her weak part for allowing the abuse or for seeking the affection of the abusive figure. That angry part will contain all the unvented rage directed at the person that caused her the most damage, especially when that damage came from the figure of attachment. Feeling rage toward that person, bonding with them would be impossible, and not forming any bonds at all is not a viable option for a child. Thus, certain memory networks won't connect with each other, because they contain totally incompatible elements. The fact that the person who takes care of us is the one who has damaged us the most is something that our mind can't assimilate. So, we form a separate compartment for each situation. When we bond with someone, we are blind to their bad side, and when we do see their bad side, we forget that this person matters to us.

As these memory networks function in a way that is not integrated, the mind will also develop into two separate areas. On one side, we will hold on to moments of bonding with the people around us. On the other side, we will harbor distrust towards the same people. We can switch from a mode of "I need affection desperately - I can't stand to be alone," to another of "I'm at war with the world - I don't need anybody." On each side, there is a radically different perspective about ourselves. We can relate with different people from each side, or we may have extremely discordant reactions towards affection or hostility when they come from the same person. It's as if a different part of us comes out, a different self, at different moments. In this way, these two aspects of our personality may form parts which have a great deal of autonomy and complexity, and which can end up functioning like two parallel minds. One of the aspects we identify with the least will be far beyond our control and awareness. As we said before, sometimes each side can control our behavior at a given time, or it can be only perceived internally.

Although this manifests itself in many different ways, let's take the example of defensive rage and the case of the fourth girl. Teresa, apart from the daily response from her parents regarding her discomfort, was bullied for several years. Of course, she never dared tell anyone at home about it, because if her mother could get so worked up about a scraped knee, she couldn't imagine how she would react to something really big. She does not expect her parents to protect her, but rather she has to protect herself from them. To do so, her body has blocked her defensive rage, and she actively separates that reaction when it comes in the face of the abuse suffered both at home and at school. This aspect of her personality gives her fear, and when she experiences rage, she feels herself reacting just like her mother, and she had sworn to herself that would never be like her. So, she tries to be an obedient child, to make everything right, and she lowers her gaze when being scolded so as not to provoke them. Rage is accumulated, but blocked and walled off. The memories of abuse will be stored in the same compartment, which has its own network of connections. In this compartment of Teresa's mind, phrases or indications of reactions arise, which rapidly try to escape. Each time, these thoughts, feelings and actions take on more pressure. By being instinctively and automatically blocked, by not allowing herself to feel them when they appear, this state is shaping a complex part of the personality. When primary school ends and the schoolmates who harassed her are no longer there, Teresa begins to hear voices in her head. These voices really come from the other side of Teresa's mind, as they are nothing other than her own thoughts. But they are so dissociated, so foreign to her, and she identifies so little with them and rejects them in such a way, that she experiences them as voices or thoughts that - she says to herself - are not hers.

Hearing voices is a more common phenomenon than it might seem, and it does not only occur in patients with psychosis or brain disorders. Of course, if it happens to us it's important that we go to a psychiatrist who can properly diagnose the problem, because they could be a result of many different underlying medical or neurological factors or psychiatric disorders, and the treatment of each of these conditions is different. But in many cases, these possible causes will be discarded, so that voices can simply be a result of traumatic experiences which we have gone through. The characteristics of these type of voices can be varied. They may be perceived clearly as voices, both inside or outside our head or as thoughts that do not seem like our own. We can see a clear relationship with the people we learned that model of functioning from; we see these voices as parts of our minds or attribute them to external entities. For example, an aggressive voice which reproduces the model of a violent father can be perceived as a monster or a demon that we carry within us. Sometimes we can even see an image that fits with that voice or that part of us as if it were outside our bodies. None of this means that we are crazy - it's simply proof that we must begin a process of reconciliation with all that is inside us, including the place where those voices or thoughts come from.

When fragmentation is very extreme, we may feel different parts within ourselves which can express themselves as internal voices or not, and with various characteristics. These parts can represent us at different ages, reflect ranges of emotions, figures in our life or other elements. There is often a conflict among these different states, which consumes our energy and causes many problems. This internal conflict among different aspects of who we are is characteristic of people who have undergone complex traumatization. There have been too many things that seemed impossible to come to terms with, even less when placed together. It's unacceptable that the people who should be taking care of us, who should consider us to be more important than anyone else, are the ones that do the most harm to us. Betrayal is the most destructive thing to the human being, as is the pain that comes from those who we have placed our trust in. This breaks us inside and profoundly alters our ability to trust other human beings. Our mind splits into pieces that we can't fit back together.

Putting these parts together again is part of the recovery process. They are all valuable. Even the most hostile voices, the parts that we reject the most, with which we identify the least, can work in our favor if we see the resources that are inside them. Once the situation that shattered our mind is over, we can look at each piece and make the best of it. From the set of each and every one of these aspects, a new definition of who we are will be born, one that will be more complete and solid. By accepting these aspects of ourselves, we won't turn out the same as the people who damaged or neglected us; on the contrary, by assimilating our more rejected aspects, we will resemble these people's models much less, and we will really begin to be ourselves.

The most hostile or critical parts can become our means of protection when we learn to use our rage to stay firm, say no, protect ourselves from the outside world and reclaim what is important to us. Although at first, these models may have been taken from aggressive, extremely demanding or controlling figures, if we embrace them and integrate them, they can evolve and change. We can express these parts in a way that has more to do with us and less to do with the people who shaped them initially.

When we start to feel safe, the smaller and more vulnerable parts will be able to connect with others and feel bonded with them. It's important that our anger does not turn against those parts and berate our "internal child" for having been vulnerable, unprotected or allowing abusive situations in our childhood. This is nothing more than reproducing in our interior the same play that we had a role in as a child. Now we have to rewrite the script.

We may experience different types of internal parts if our mind is quite fragmented. Some of these parts may be related to a period of time or a memory, or they may reproduce what someone important to us might have done, or represent what we would like to be, and so on. In any case, its symbolic meaning is clear to us. Even in the cases where some parts do not seem to be related to us, or we don't see connections with our experiences, they will always end up making sense if we look at them in a new light, keeping our whole past in mind. For example, we can have a part of ourselves, like a child, that represents what we were until our life changed. Sometimes we may feel like that excited little girl or hear her voice in our head. Somehow our mind preserved that state that defined us for many years, although we believed we lost it. There may be a part that denies that our memories really happened or that argues that we are not ill or that we don't have problems. If we had to go forward through the war in which we grew up, acting as if nothing happened or as if it had nothing to do with us, it is an adaptive reaction. Some parts may represent different ages or moments in our life, since in those moments things happened that interrupted our development. We move forward, but it's as if a part of us remains stuck in that time. The memory of what happened, the severity of it, or the emotions linked to it can be stored in that blocked memory network, and become accessible only when we connect with that state. It doesn't matter whether these appear in the form of voices, thoughts or impulses in our mind, they have a meaning. On the road to recovery, we must reconcile with everything we have held within us. The stranger, more alien and aberrant those parts seem, the more relevant the process of reconciliation with those aspects is.

Of course, finding the healthy functioning of each part, the meaning behind the voices we hear, the thoughts or impulses we feel, is not easy. But there are some questions that we can ask ourselves that will help. Here are some examples:

Who do the voices or thoughts in our head or the parts we feel inside resemble? If they leave behind what they were modeled on, could they evolve and accomplish the same thing in a different way?

For example, we might hear our ex-husband - who was repeatedly abusive to us - insulting us. It's not just a memory of words once said to us, because sometimes they are said with regard to things that we do in the present. This voice calls us useless and tells us that we are worthless, in a strong, hard, authoritarian voice that is full of anger. It resembles our ex-husband, but it's not him, it's us. This toughness, that extreme rage, would be good if we made it our own and didn't allow anyone to treat us that way. This will probably be difficult because hearing it will scare us, since we were frightened when we were with that person, but we won't remind ourselves of that because it's in our mind, that voice is ours, and it may be possible to differentiate it from the initial mold that shaped it, and turn it into something else. It can come and join us on our side.

What emotion is predominant in that part? Why do we humans have such a range of emotions? How could we feel and express those emotions? What changes could we make to achieve this?

We experience a thought that tells us that we should die. We don't actually want to do it; in fact, we should fight against that urge. It's a feeling, that of a little girl, and if we try to imagine her, she is seven years old and bowing her head in shame. We try to remember, and think about what happened when we were seven, and realize that at that stage there had been a couple of incidents of sexual abuse at the hands of a neighbor in our building. We have never disclosed this to anyone, and today we tell ourselves that it's not important, but either way we should check if there is still any sensation associated with that memory. We stop to think about that event and it seems neutral, but we examine this seven-year-old girl for a while, and see what feelings come. After a minute, we begin to feel some shame, and our first impulse is to avoid the girl's gaze. But we know that shame in and of itself is not bad, that surely at that time, being so small, the girl we were did not know what to do, and that feeling was extremely disturbing for her. It had to be very strange and distressing to keep a secret like this. It's normal for us to try to get rid of the shame, and that that shame becomes associated with a lot of fear and discomfort. Now that we are adults, we can reconnect with these feelings and understand them, as if for the first time someone understood what was happening to that little girl and would relay to her that there is nothing wrong with her, that the man who did that to her was the bad one, and that it was not her fault. We notice the shame coming out of the memory and reaching the consciousness, but keep our head high and look forward. To keep the emotion with us, when we go back to the memory and talk about it with others, we leave the present to air out those old memories, and thereby water down the related feelings. Beliefs and thoughts come, like a sensation of feeling dirty, bad or different, but we remind ourselves that these beliefs are part of the memory, and it is normal for them to emerge. We understand that from all those feelings that we bury, a desire to disappear also springs up. Then everything starts to make sense, and we feel calm. We don't really want to die; we only felt this in a very desperate moment of our lives, and one part of us was trapped in that experience. Luckily, we did not die, and now we can fix it. We can rescue that stuck part and bring it into the present, where things are different. Although we were faced with similar situations in the past, everything has changed because our situation is quite different now: we are adults, we are wiser, and we can protect ourselves. And if in addition we start talking about all those experiences with normality, to people who we know can understand us, the old feelings will dissipate further.

What do we notice when we look into our mind or draw a mental image of that part, that thought or that voice on a piece of paper? What do we feel that this part needs? How can we give it - and therefore give ourselves - what it needs?

The voice is shapeless; it only says that we won't be able to do anything, whispering to us, "You're useless." When we try to do something, it's always there, blocking our actions. Thinking about this, we take a piece of paper and draw the first thing that comes to mind. What we get can be something without a clear meaning, like a worm. This feeling seems familiar to us, so we try to remember if we have felt it before. Our mind goes back to school, to the children who bullied us for years. That experience left us completely stuck, unable to do anything, and we could not study. In exams, our mind would go blank and we would fail almost all of them. At home nobody realized what was happening to us; they believed that we were just lazy and reacted by putting more pressure on us. The feeling of being useless, of being insignificant, just like a worm, was constant at that stage.

After some time, we overcame that situation and changed schools, and then in high school, we acted as if nothing had happened. We behaved in a completely different way, changed the type of friends we had, and made a radical turn. Those patterns of behavior of that stage stayed behind, but they did not disappear. We did many things in life, achieved many things, and we felt capable. But that little worm represents a part of us that stayed behind. It's as if that portion of our minds was not aware of all that we have achieved in life, because the change was too fast and did not have time to evolve. We look at the picture we drew, think about the person we were when those feelings predominated, and remind ourselves that we can do many things, that we are capable, and that not everything in our life has been like that.

Around the initial representation we draw all the experiences and people who conveyed different things to us. Little by little, the drawing changes, as do our internal feelings. What we needed at the time was precisely this: someone who could see beyond all of it, realize what was happening to us, and say, "I trust you, I know you can deal with it," both encouraging and protecting us at the same time. Although it did not happen then, we are still in time to repair our feelings now.

We don't let ourselves get confused by the apparent behavior of these parts. Our impulses may bring negative consequences, but what do they ultimately seek? How can we achieve this without causing ourselves problems?

This is the worst of our voices or thoughts; it shouts and confounds us, and we become terrified when we hear it. It's like an inner monster that wants to destroy us, something that wants to bring us to its side and coerce us in to doing bad things. But we know that it's a part of ourselves, and it's very difficult to imagine that any good can come of it, but because it pertains to our mind, it must contain something vital for us. Our system has preserved it, and it's still there for some reason. We have been struggling for years against it, and the stronger the fight is, the worse everything goes. It's necessary to go beyond its terrifying appearance and face what is behind it.

We listen to what that part says, let it write in our diary, and we see that in the midst of all the insults, it warns us about our current partner. The relationship has problems, but we feel that it's our fault for having frequent outbursts of anger. When that part dominates us, we can't control ourselves. Sometimes we punch a wall so we don't hit someone. In that state, we only want to dominate, to crush, and we don't feel any love for the other person.

But we reflect on the sequences, on what happens before our outbursts. We realize that the most intolerable issue for us is that our partner tells us what we should do. To be honest, somehow it's as if we provoke the altercation, because we always leave everything to the last minute, or we "forget," so the other person has to repeatedly remind us about our responsibilities, and we become more and more annoyed. Usually we see the avalanche coming from the beginning, but do not do anything to stop it. Are we familiar with these feelings?

Our mother was a very dominant woman who was harsh and authoritarian. When she gave us a beating, we could see hate in her eyes, and she looked completely out of control. When we grew up, we could face her and hit her back. The only way to stop her aggression was to respond with the same violence. In some way it's as if we provoke our partner to end up being insistent and brusque, as if we push her to follow the same script and to adopt the complementary role. The mind is curious and drifts to the familiar routes, as if trying to retrace our steps in order to give it another end, but paradoxically ending up repeating it.

Our overflowing rage protected us in our teens, and in some way, it stopped everything. All of the accumulated pain gave rise to an uncontrollable reaction, but as much as the rage goes out, the pain does not go away. We are aware of it now and stop to realize. Actually, the most painful thing was not the beatings, but rather the lack of love we felt from our mother. We clung to our rage, because it was the only possible connection with her. And now, living with a partner who loves us, we don't know how to behave without returning to that pattern, to the first template of how attachment bonds were formed. We understand our inner monster, we can see what is inside, understand the pain and the terrible affective deprivation that we carry. It's then that we can begin to change it, stop the automatic functioning, become aware and take the reins. The beginning of the sequence is that we are not carrying out our responsibilities, so we focus on doing these things so that our spouse no longer has grounds to reproach us. We are also going to guide our partner regarding the way they say things, so they do not irritate us so much, and so we can be more receptive. We talk about the experiences we had and how they affected us. We are patient with each other, and we work towards change.

Rather than trying to set aside whatever comes to our mind, such as the thoughts, voices or impulses that overwhelm us, we must learn to listen to them, to take note of ourselves and how we feel, and to understand every aspect and nuance of who we are. Sometimes we are so concerned about trying to control what we notice or push it away, that we don't know how to stop to understand and establish a dialogue with ourselves. For this reason, it's important not to let ourselves be guided by the apparent behavior, because usually things are not what they seem. As with any dialogue that we intend to engage in after a long conflict, it's important to be open, listen and redirect the conversation that will often return to the same old argument. We must change our prejudices and question our beliefs. The greatest enemies can become allies when they form a team that cooperates to reach a common goal. This collaboration among our internal tendencies is easier, because we must not forget that everything that is in our head belongs to us. Everything, even the most foreign or unpleasant aspects, are "us" in the broadest sense of the word. One day all these parts will understand that we are in the same boat, and that by fighting for the rudder, the boat is navigating in circles. We realize that the deep objective, which was initially unknown, is a shared goal, because human tendency will always be towards our collective well-being and the establishment of meaningful relationships. There is so much to do, so it's important to get to it.

If we are reading this chapter and we recognize ourselves in it, if we feel that there are many parts within ourselves, fighting to define who we are, this process that we are explaining will be very hard to do without the help of specialized professionals. If we are surrounded by healthy people, of course they will be an important source of support, and if we are determined to change things, we have the key to make those changes. Psychotherapy is an additional resource that does not negate the importance and usefulness of these others, but is usually necessary to guide us in the process.

10 WHO WINS IN THE FIGHT AGAINST OURSELVES?

I learned to make my mind large, as the universe is large, so that there is room for paradoxes. Maxine Hong Kingston.

Would a fight between our right hand and our left make sense? We can do so much more with both hands instead of just one. Why limit our possibilities? Why choose between being vulnerable and protecting ourselves? Why decide whether our rational part is better than our emotional part, or only feel some of our emotions, when we have a more complete palette of colors? However, we often act this way, without realizing that it's not only counterproductive for us, but that it's also impossible.

We can't suppress any part of ourselves, precisely because it's there and it's ours. Any attempt to remove, reject, avoid, bury or anesthetize an aspect of who we are often paradoxically leads to the opposite of what we are looking for. That part remains within us, and in addition, we disrupt its possibility to grow and evolve into a different version of itself. If it continues to operate rigidly from the old patterns, we remain unable to react when faced with circumstances that we should be able to handle without any problems. Only by recovering each element of who we are, freeing them from their constraints and letting them evolve, can we get the change we seek.

As said before, this rejection of certain aspects of our personality usually has its origin in the history of our significant relationships. We see ourselves as we have been seen by others. But once this image of ourselves is internalized, it becomes our own perspective, and we can lose track of how it developed. We simply believe that things are this way and that it's not possible to feel differently.

This internal conflict is nothing more than a dilemma[19]: a false choice between opposites. To put it another way, it's as if we fixate on trying to decide whether to choose the letter A or Z instead of writing with the whole alphabet. It's obvious that we need all the letters and that there is no possible solution to the question we ask. The solution is to change the question.

The new question is: What's good about this part of me that I dislike? As impossible as it may seem, there is always something good deep within; there is always a healthy function for which this part was originally designed. It was all the molding that we and the environment gave to it that made it take on the shape that it has now. The first molding was done by the external people we lived with, but we have helped to maintain that part exactly as it was molded. It's our rejection of it, the conflict with that aspect of our personality, which is not allowing it to develop. Without the conflict that we have with ourselves, the material that part is made of is like clay, which can change its shape completely. We just have to help it evolve.

How can we do that? It's both very simple and very complex. Because every part of us needs thc same things we all need in order to grow, develop, and give our best: to be looked upon with unconditional love. The essential thing is that someone sees us in the deep sense of the word and accepts us like this, with our limitations, and is able to realize who we are and who we can become. Therefore, when we are able to look at each part of ourselves with new eyes, understand it, take care of and accept it, even what we find most alien can be integrated, and begin to evolve. When we become adults, the gaze that really counts is our own, the one that we direct towards ourselves.

Our aggressive part

For example, if we have rage that we won't accept, a side with more complex anger that sometimes controls us or an aggressive voice in our head that insults us or that pushes us to do things that we don't want to do, our starting point should be that this part is there for a good reason and that it's possible to understand how it developed. We can look back and understand what models this part has learned from. We will also see later how this rage continued accumulating within us, as we experience similar situations, which we could not face otherwise because we were emotionally blocked from the beginning.

Often people who grew up in complex environments say, "OK, yes, I was a child then and I couldn't do anything.... But ever since I have been reacting the same way, and I can't forgive myself for that." The element that we are forgetting is that when rage is not accepted and integrated, it does not actually protect us adequately. If it lashes out of control or if we swallow it, torturing ourselves, this emotion will not work in our favor because we are fighting against it, because we are not a team. If we always try to control our rage, whatever the situation, even when feeling it would be logical and healthy, we can end up enduring negative situations for too long. We may try to avoid getting angry for fear of exploding, or we may not solve problems because we can't tolerate conflict or don't know how to handle confrontations; we are afraid of the anger of others and so we withhold ours. But that unexpressed anger accumulates every day, and we may end up losing control and exploding, creating so much internal tension that we become physically ill.

To change this, we need new models. We can follow the example of the people that we know who feel their rage differently, who can be firm when necessary, and who can be undisturbed and not lose control. They know how to say "No," and they know how to protect themselves when others try to hurt them. Our rage can learn from these types of functioning, instead of remaining stuck in the worst models. When it does, this emotion will be on our side and protect us. It will regain the protective function for which it was designed, use it to our advantage, and it will give the best of itself. It will be very different from the external models of uncontrolled and harmful anger. We will feel our rage as ours.

Our vulnerable part

In the same way, we can reconcile with our most vulnerable parts, with our sadness, and with the painful emotions that we felt in certain moments of our lives. We had to disconnect ourselves from this part, because feeling all of that would have meant being unable to move forward. Our feelings may even remind us of the pain of some significant people in our past, and we find it hard to see it both in ourselves and in other people. We don't know how to deal with it and what to do with all those sensations.

The main problem of setting aside our most vulnerable part is that nobody can actually see us, and we can't truly connect to other people. And even if we say that it's better that way, that if we don't let anyone really see us or don't establish deep ties, nobody can harm us again, the truth is that we damage ourselves much more than anyone else has. We deprive ourselves of air and drown within the walls that we have built to protect us. Of all the experiences that a person can go through, the most destructive is undoubtedly that important people in our life were incapable of tuning into and understanding our needs. This lack of connection is the most damaging and internally - in a paradoxical way - we can end up doing something similar by disconnecting and isolating ourselves from others.

Let's, once again, use a healthy point of reference. There are people who seek out connections with others, despite knowing that those we establish emotional ties with can disappoint us. They accept the pain that sometimes comes with what life brings. They just take care of their pain until it goes away, and then move forward. It's true that if our environment has been problematic, we won't have many models of this type that can serve as a healthy point of reference, but if we look closely, we will find some examples among the people we know. From them we can start to reformulate our way of working, and our vulnerable part can learn from them.

Our caregiver part

Children try to feel some sort of control in their relationships when their bonds are disorganized and no longer safe. They can become aggressive with their caregivers or focus instead on taking care of them. This is common when caregivers are constantly sick, anxious or depressed, and are unable to meet the needs of their children. In this situation, the children are the ones who will adopt a caregiver role. These children may then continue to relate to others from a caregiving perspective, establishing the same pattern in most of their relationships.

If we recognize ourselves in this pattern, we probably have a highly-developed caregiver part. We throw ourselves at others, paying little attention to our own needs. We may feel more comfortable caring for others than being cared for, although internally, the unfulfilled longing for love, attention and satisfaction that every child has, is still inside us. Now, we rarely receive this affection and attention, since we tend to surround ourselves with people who fit in with our caregiving role and tend to let themselves be cared for or seek our attention. Additionally, if someone tries to help or take care of us, our system is not prepared for such a position, and we may feel uncomfortable, distrust others or not allow ourselves to take that position. The problem with mainly establishing ties as a caregiver is that this is not a fully satisfactory relationship (although it may seem so) but is instead a substitute for a truly healthy connection with others. Lacking good attachment bonds, we cannot internalize a pattern of self-regulation and self-care that allows us to be autonomous in relation to others, and we may feel that if we don't take care of others, we are nothing. It's true that if we do not work on restoring our internal system, we won't know how to define ourselves otherwise.

If we recognize ourselves in this operating pattern, we most likely have a very developed caregiver part, and this is not usually a rejected one. People functioning this way often identify with the role of a caregiver. From this point, reaching exhaustion is very common, since we give others everything they ask for and more, constantly ignoring our own needs in order to satisfy someone else's. At an emotional level, we expend more energy than we take in. We may realize that something is wrong, feel bad in some way for being like that, and slightly decrease our level of involvement with others out of pure exhaustion. However, the pattern continues to run in the background, and we continue having the strong belief that we have to dedicate ourselves to others completely, and as a result, we get upset when people do not respond as we expect them to. We are also angry because we must give up, deny or bury many of our own needs, in order to make sacrifices for others. If we stopped to notice that underlying rage, we could not continue functioning in a caregiver role, but that unconscious rage may turn into resentment, bitterness and dissatisfaction. Without realizing it, we can reproach people we expect gratitude from, for example, by complaining about how little they come to see us when they do. Although we don't say anything, our non-verbal language will end up distancing others from us. Our gestures, as much as we try to cover them up, transmit the message to other people that they are not doing things correctly or sufficiently. This feeling, however, does not inspire them to increase their gratitude and care, and if they do display gratitude, it won't be spontaneous but forced. We are all stuck in a spider web, and the more we move, the more trapped we become. If we identify these three parts - aggressive, vulnerable and caregiver - the process of change requires the three of them to remain but change the way in which they are oriented. Our rage must stop turning inward in the form of a demand or attack on ourselves. We will stop insulting ourselves for being vulnerable or weak, and forcing ourselves to care for others. This rage will turn outward, to fulfill its role of protecting us from those who want us to do harm, and fight for what we need. Our caregiver part, on the other hand, must turn inward. This way it will help us take better care of ourselves, see our needs and meet them. Thus, the pain will diminish, the feeling of emotional deprivation will go away, and we will prevent further damage by protecting ourselves better. As we can see, a healthy system consists of the same parts, only arranged in a different way.

All this may have multiple nuances, as we can notice internally very different reactions among conflicting internal parts. We can feel rejection, fear, rage or shame in the presence of some of them. The process in every case is the same: whatever the part of us that we dislike, there is always a hidden chance for development. Without integrating all the parts that we have inside ourselves, we won't be complete, just as our body would not be if we tried to live without lungs or a heart. Each organ has a vital function that none other can do; the same is true at the psychological level. Seeing the resources that are within us, in the most hidden, rejected, and least recognized parts, is essential to living well. The different aspects are not contradictory, but complementary; they balance each other out. Every aspect of our personality is a key element, which, when combined with others, modulates our internal functioning and the way we move through life. Each part has distinct elements of reality, a piece of our past, and an ingredient for what is happening now. In each of them there is a valuable resource. The work we need to do is to discover this valuable resource, unblock each part, move them from conflict to collaboration, from fight to negotiation, from competing with each other to forming a team. It's a question of multiplying forces, energy and resources, not of dividing them. If we come to a fork in the road and cannot choose which way to go, it does not make any sense for each of our parts to be pulling in opposite directions. It's better to sit down, share ideas, get advice if we don't know how to move forward, and ask for help or search for tools if what we have is insufficient; once a strategy is settled on, we can push all our parts in the same direction. The time spent doing this is not wasted time. When a team is capable of coordinating their efforts like this, they function much more smoothly when it becomes necessary.

11 PROTECTING MYSELF

I suppose it is tempting, if the only tool you have is a hammer, to treat everything as if it were a nail. Abraham Maslow.

When we put a rabbit and a cat on their backs, with their bellies exposed, we can see two very different reactions. A cat that does not see us as a threat, allows us to pet its tummy, and appears completely relaxed. It purrs and wiggles, reacting positively to physical contact. The rabbit, by contrast, remains motionless, with stiff legs and fixed eyes. It enters a kind of trance-like state in which it is still and rigid, but not relaxed.

Why is there such a difference? Rabbits eat vegetables, and in the food chain, they are at the bottom: usually they are the prey. When they feel threatened, they keep still because, as explained in previous chapters, feigning death makes the predator lose interest. This reaction readily occurs, because rabbits feel threatened easily. Thanks to their fear, they are cautious and careful, and this strategy has helped them survive. For an animal like a rabbit - lacking the body size of a bear or the teeth of a lion - fear that drives it to escape at full speed, and immobility when it's captured are both effective instincts that have allowed the survival of the species. The largest and most ferocious dinosaurs were not so fortunate.

On the other hand, felines are predators, and even when they live in a domestic environment, they continue to maintain the same reactions. The cat lets us pet it because it has teeth and claws and knows how to use them. If the person approaching is perceived as a threat, the cat will flaunt its weapons by flashing its teeth and claws. With its master or human family, it leaves its claws inside fluffy little pads which are nice to touch. It can go from purring mode to scratching and biting in milliseconds, so even on its back, the cat feels totally safe. The cat allows itself to be in such a vulnerable position because it knows very well that it can protect itself.

We humans are heirs of all the species that came before us. Our brain reacts in ways that are similar to those of reptiles and others present in lower mammals and primates. For this reason, our repertoire of protective systems covers a wide range of possibilities which our nervous system activates in an instinctive way, depending on the perception of the threat and the possibilities we have to defend ourselves in each specific situation.

When we are children, we have no other option but to function like rabbits. Like them, we are not as big as adults, nor do we have their strength and authority. Within our families and schools, we have nowhere to go or no one to turn to except to those who take care of us. It will be a long time until we are physically and emotionally self-sufficient, both in terms of our self-care and the regulation of our emotions. Our body knows that perfectly well, and when faced with aggression at home or at school, the responses of immobility, of being paralyzed, and of obeying are the best possible defense options. Would it make any sense for a rabbit to fight a lion? It's unthinkable, so instinctively, our nervous system rules this option out.

However, there is also a cat within us; the basis of the reactions that we will be able to perform as adults is already rooted in our nervous system. Therefore, the fight response is activated, but it's instinctively blocked sometimes even before we are aware of it. This is another reason that explains why rage gets blocked when we are faced with a situation of hostility or aggression, whether it's physical or emotional. Also, fear and the escape reaction are activated and blocked. In childhood or in situations with no way out, such as being trapped in a warzone or physically or emotionally abducted, our automatic protective reactions are activated and are immediately suppressed, without our noticing them, since in these circumstances they wouldn't have been useful to us.

This fact is important for many people who blame themselves for not leaving or for not fighting when faced with an adverse situation. We are not weaker for not using these systems if we don't have the advantage; we are simply acting through the wisdom of our species and all those who have come before us. It does not make sense to blame ourselves for not being adults before adulthood, for having not grown up before we have had the time to do so.

Fight and flight responses can become permanently blocked. After the problematic situation ends, and we are faced with similar events in other stages of our life - when active reaction responses would be possible and adaptive - its activation also triggers the old blockage. We could already fight, say no, and stand firm when others say things that bother us, but because of our blocked system we cannot react or are afraid to do so. We could change partners, find another job, distance ourselves from our parents, or connect with other people, but we are prisoners in those relationships as if we were still a small child without options. We could protect ourselves, but we feel unprotected.

The human brain also has a highly developed capacity for reflective thinking that is less present in other species. We can think about what happens to us and try responses beyond the instinctively programmed ones. But in threatening situations, there is no time for that, and we turn back to primal, automatic reactions. It's a matter of survival. Sometimes, in serious situations or continuous trauma, our rational side can work against us, harshly judging us for not having reacted, blaming us for allowing something to happen or pressuring us to overcome our blockage. The effect of doing this, instead of untying the knot, only makes it tighter. When there are problems with attachment relationships in childhood, the ability to reflect on what we feel and do later in life will be greatly affected. Human beings, with our sophisticated nervous system, also generate much more elaborate protection responses. Our mind always tries to protect us from what it perceives as a threat, even those that we notice within ourselves. When we have grown up or spent a lot of time in a threatening or hostile environment, we can develop many mechanisms to neutralize the damage, become permanently defensive or have blocked reactions that function rigidly. In either case, we don't protect ourselves in way that is appropriate and proportionate to each situation. But even if these systems are activated at the wrong time, in the wrong place, or in a way that is disproportionate to the situation, they are still, in essence, protective systems. At other times in our life, they were the best or the only ones possible.

Let's examine different reactions, which, broadly speaking, can be understood as ways in which we can protect ourselves. Some of them are our instinctive defensive reactions which get triggered despite their blockage. Others are substitutes we turn to when we can't defend ourselves from danger that comes from interpersonal relationships or when we can't face our own feelings. It's important, as we commented before, to develop more self-awareness and understand how these reactions can be activated by different external triggers or internal emotional states. These defensive responses are part of the sequences that we described previously, but they are not core feelings, but rather reactions to them. Some of these will be further described below.

I am the only one who…

I have values that others don't have. I am the only one who truly says things as they are. I'm the only one who actually cares about things or other people. I am the only one who cares about doing things right. Sometimes I don't say it like this - since it's not politically correct to do so - but when I tell myself that people are selfish, that nobody cares about anyone else, and that people have no values, I am implicitly saying that I am the exception or one of the few people in the world that do.

People owe me

The world owes me for everything that has happened to me. People need to understand me, and they have to support me. They must be there when I need them. I don't say it as if I were demanding it of others, rather as if it were a matter of justice, as if everyone that I meet has the obligation to give me what I've been denied. I hear myself, either aloud or silently, finding fault with others for how they treat me.

I am dominant

I enjoy the sensation of winning, surpassing others. I get hooked on competition and in a contest, finishing second is the same as coming in last. In relationships, I have to be the one in control, the one who leads. Having power is the best feeling in the world. I think I am worthy of leading other people. In some areas this is valued, but sometimes I don't openly show it or even recognize myself.

I am superior

I am much better than others at some things, although they do not always give me enough credit for it. Sometimes people envy me for this reason. It bothers me that people who are worth much less than I am get ahead of me, but I usually don't say anything because it's inappropriate. I tend to comment on it when others fail, so I may indirectly stand out among less capable people who know less than I do. If we see flaws in everybody, it's likely that - without realizing it - we reveal this tendency.

I distrust

I constantly expect others to let me down; I am attuned to any small signs of this, and as soon as I see them, I rule that person out completely and confirm my negative predictions. Sometimes I look for evidence of the anticipated betrayal or test others. I have a scanner that is constantly working, I never relax or let my guard down. I believe that everyone has bad intentions and that in this life, there is no one I can rely on.

I submit

I surrender control to others or accept things I do not want, in order to avoid conflicts, reprisals or abandonment. Faced with the demands of another, I am always the one who gives in. If anyone imposes on me, I keep my head down and try to please that person. I tell myself that I don't like conflicts, so I do what other people tell me to do or support their opinions, although I don't believe in them. I can even doubt what I really think and take on someone else's perspective.

I sacrifice

My priority is to satisfy the needs of others by sacrificing mine. The most important thing is the wellbeing of others and preventing their suffering. I feel selfish if I do things for my own benefit or don't care for others. I do whatever I have to make others happy. I think that their wellbeing is my responsibility, and that my needs don't matter or should be secondary.

I am indispensable

I am convinced that things only go forward when I am in charge. I think that unless I control everything, things will either not get done or will be done poorly. In the end, I have to do everything on my own, because no matter how much I supervise the work of others, there is no point. It's more trouble for me to worry about how others are doing things than just to do them myself.

I control myself

I constantly have to control my feelings, what I think or what I do. I bury my emotions or get angry with myself for feeling a certain way. If I stopped controlling everything, it would just turn into chaos, and would be overwhelmed - this is something that I try to avoid at all costs. I tell myself what I should and shouldn't feel, and it can't be any other way. I crush my feelings, drown my desires, and push them down, inwards. Everything needs to be under control, things need to be predictable, so that I know what to expect. I try to avoid uncertainty, because I don't deal with it well

I'm so demanding that I drive myself into the ground

I put too much pressure on myself. I don't tolerate my mistakes, not even one, and I must do my very best. Everything I have to do comes above my own needs, and I have to reach the highest possible level. I must be perfect and do everything well. No matter how much or how well I do it, it is never enough, and I have to keep doing more and more. I often wind up exhausted; sometimes it's impossible to keep the bar so high for myself, but lowering it seems unacceptable to me.

I can't deal with unfairness

I don't accept the idea that people who make mistakes or don't do things well shouldn't suffer as a result. I get very angry when people don't fulfill their duties. I don't tolerate things done incorrectly. I can't stand injustice or informality - I refuse to overlook those situations. I am pleased when people who do things badly get what they deserve, and I think this is what should always happen.

I shut myself down inside

So that no one gets too close and hurts me, I build a wall that no one can get through. I try to make it so that other people don't affect me; I don't get involved in their problems, nor do I let them get to know me. My walls are made of many materials: rejecting others, questioning their attempts to approach me or doing things that I know will push them away. I shut down personal questions or avoid letting people approach me. I always keep a distance, my relationships are superficial, and I end them or leave if they reach a level of greater intimacy. I see the world from a distance, trying to live on the edge.

I attack

I react aggressively. I jump on or attack other people. I can criticize, insult, and shout. I also have less violent reactions such as making hurtful comments or no longer talking to the person who bothers me. In any of those forms, I hurt others as a response to the damage they did to me or to preempt anticipated damage. Sometimes I attack first so as not to let others to take advantage of me, or I attack when faced with any attitude that I find annoying or threatening. Sometimes I react so quickly that I am not even aware of what really triggers me.

I crush myself

I blame myself internally for feeling bad, for doing things I do, for thinking what I think. Sometimes I feel guilty for existing in the world. If other people blame or judge me, I can't stand it. It's terrible for me, but the most ruthless criticism comes from myself.

I take care of everybody around me

I throw myself into the care of others because it makes me feel good. I take care of people because this is how I am, and it comes naturally for me. In many relationships, this is the role that I perform. Although people don't thank me for this, or I know that I will end up exhausted, I can't change my tendency. Taking on another role, such as taking care of myself, is difficult for me and when I have no other choice because I am sick or just not okay, I don't handle it well. Sometimes it hurts that others don't appreciate everything I do for them or when they don't even thank me for it.

I rely on the devil I know

When I am in a bad mood or annoyed, and others try to help or encourage me, I feel misunderstood, because they don't realize just how bad I am. If they try to help me, I push them away. I don't think about making changes because I can't change how I am, and in my circumstances, it's impossible to be okay. I am convinced of what I think about myself, other people and the world, and although those beliefs cause me discomfort, I don't try to change them because I'm sure I'm right. If I stop a while to think about what it would be like to feel okay, I get uncomfortable with the idea. It's as if I can't allow myself to feel good, as if I were afraid or did not have the right to change. I prefer not to delude myself into thinking that I'll get better, in order to keep from being disappointed. Even when things are looking up, I think that there is something bad just around the corner.

I pretend

My face does not reflect what I feel inside me. I show what I believe I am supposed to express or what I believe is expected of me. I tend to hide my emotions, so that no one can see my intentions or my needs. I adapt my actions to what I assume should be done or simply try to appear normal. Sometimes I don't know how I am supposed to feel, so I am guided by others' behaviors, so that I go unnoticed.

I complain

My thoughts revolve around the bad things that happen to me or what others have done to me in the past. I'm constantly thinking about my problems, always stuck in an endless loop and never reaching a conclusion. I think about difficult situations, but not about the solutions that I might have for them. After someone says or does something that bothers me, the situation is continuously played in a loop in my head. I regret my bad luck.

I withstand everything

Since I can, I tend to take on everything. I'm strong, and I never lean on other people. I function in a self-reliant way in every situation, which means I don't like to ask for help. No matter the burden or its weight, I never share it. I don't need anything or anyone.

I idealize

I always have a very positive image of others, of my ability to solve a problem or of what I'm like as a person. I see things, people or myself, just as I would like them to be. It's hard for me to recognize that relevant figures in my life may have flaws or defects. I change reality to make it match the version in my head. Sometimes I live on my own planet, where everything is as it should be. In my world, alternate versions of people live there, and they behave towards me the way I want them to. The family that I wanted to have lives on that planet; it's always where my dream job, my soulmate and my true friends are. I spend all day comparing reality with my ideal world. I solve problems with theoretical solutions that don't apply to my real situation and imagine myself in a future without difficulties, where everything is easy.

I am numb

I don't feel things that other people might feel in the same situations. Sometimes I feel my emotions disappearing or ceasing to exist. I may not notice physical or emotional pain, or it may suddenly disappear, voluntarily or automatically. Sometimes it's as if I had no feelings at all. When interior numbness does not work, I turn to do things in order not to feel or block out my thoughts or memories; I do this by drinking, taking medication or doing drugs. I distract myself with lots of activities and by doing risky things that require all my attention.

I avoid

I steer clear of what bothers or scares me, and those things that I feel I can't handle. Sometimes I put it all off until the last minute, until there is no other choice. I give all kinds of excuses, and although they are all quite similar, and deep inside I know that I am tricking myself, I use them as reasons for not doing so. I say to myself that I can't, and without really checking to see if it's true, I believe it literally. I may also find something else that I deem more urgent and give it a higher priority, and this way I have a compelling reason not to deal with the problem. I might consciously avoid things, or get mentally or physically ill, and then I feel that I have a fair pretext for not doing so.

I give up

Sometimes I throw in the towel, let myself go, and do things that make me feel even worse; although I am aware of what I'm doing, I don't stop it. When the downward spiral starts, I drop the reins and let myself be dragged along. I say to myself, "I can't do it," and believe this without questioning it. I think, "I don't feel like it" and even if it's something good or necessary for me, I decide that the only possible option is doing whatever I feel like doing at the moment. I don't reflect on the negative consequences of doing it, I just tell myself that I can't stop doing it, I get swept up. I throw myself on the sled, with my hands off the brakes. Sometimes even when I hit rock bottom, I continue digging. I think that giving up is less painful than fighting for nothing. It's not worth it.

Some of these reactions are instinctive protection mechanisms. Attacking has to do with the fight defense, avoidance is related to escape, and submission is the only available resource when active responses are not viable. In situations where there are no options, numbing our emotions makes painful sensations tolerable. Think back on the rabbit and its trance-like state when it was exposed in a vulnerable position. All of them are reactions related to survival when faced with a perceived threat, and they are present in many animal species. The activation of one these systems is usually quick and automatic and occurs long before we can consciously reflect on what is happening.

In other cases, rather than a means of protection against external elements, these instinctive defenses can be better understood as mechanisms to regulate our emotions, for example, the use of control. Some are compensatory systems, addressing the lack of an attachment bond that makes us feel protected, such as performing a caregiver role. What these all have in common is that they are systems that do not lead to real regulation or to adaptive relationships with other people and our surroundings. Like a spare tire, they are acceptable in emergency systems, but frequently they continue to be active after the actual emergency, and become automatic responses or permanent patterns. For example, as previously mentioned, escape is an excellent protection for a rabbit when the door is open, but if it runs away from the person who brings it food or is coming to help it, fleeing becomes a problem. In the same way for humans, avoidance is a psychological mechanism that makes us more and more afraid of difficulties, and they become increasingly greater.

These reactions can be automatic or quite conscious. We can identify with them or feel them as attitudes that spring from within, but that we don't like or understand. As we mentioned, the tendency to take care of others can be part of how we define ourselves as individuals. It's possible that we have even looked for a profession or a social situation in which this role fits perfectly. Additionally, at a cultural level, generosity and altruism have a positive connotation. It might be difficult to realize that we ultimately expect gratitude or reciprocity, because that would mean that we are looking for it, and this would introduce an element in the way we see ourselves that might be difficult to accept. However, the disappointment we feel when those that we take care of do not show us gratitude implies that somehow, we hoped it wouldn't be like that.

The same may happen with some of the other systems, regarding their social and moral worth. For example, being dominant and competitive can be a positive value in some business environments. Enjoying the feeling of being on top can be an asset for an attorney. If we are part of a street gang or group of troubled kids at school, being aggressive will give us status in the eyes of our peers. In a political party, a demanding attitude can be understood as a strong ideological conviction. In a religious congregation, taking care of and sacrificing oneself for others would be considered a moral objective. Our own concepts or standards, and the unwritten rules in each family can make some functioning styles harder to recognize and accept as unhealthy. However, it's very important for us to be able to identify them within ourselves. Remember that the things we are not conscious of operate in a more powerful way than what we perceive clearly. We can only change the things that we know exist.

How do we identify these reactions if we are deceiving ourselves? An indirect indicator is to think about things that we can't stand in others. Logically, we prefer some behaviors over others. However, when there are features that we don't tolerate in other people or ourselves, it most likely has to do with our history and how we are. What we reject viscerally in others is somehow present in our inner world. For example, it can bother us a lot when people criticize or discredit others, to the point of staying very upset and thinking about the incident over and over again. Interestingly, when this happens, it's common for us to criticize ourselves a lot internally, saying things like, "I'm an idiot, I am not worth anything, I do everything wrong, I'm a disaster." Therefore, the criticism from others multiplies when it touches us inside, like a sounding board. The most ruthless critic is inside us, but we are only aware of what comes from the outside. Our internal mental processes are too close, and at the same time overly blocked.

Nevertheless, in all the reactions that were described in this chapter, there is a potential resource. Feeling that we are above others could compensate for - and is probably the reason why it develops - a deep feeling of being undervalued. Control is fine when we apply it to situations that we can handle, although it gives us problems if we try to use it for things that don't work well with control, such as emotions, or that are beyond our control, such as unexpected events or situations. As discussed above, no human reaction is completely maladjusted, and always has to do with a healthy function. Finding that function and modulating our response is our goal. The problem comes when there are extreme, unregulated, or out of context reactions. The basis of mental health is balance and flexibility. With a broad, versatile and flexible repertoire of conduct, our ability to effectively deal with situations will always be greater.

Therefore, if we find any of these protection systems inside ourselves, we must ask ourselves a few questions:

1. What am I protecting myself from?

2. Where did I learn to protect myself this way?

3. Is this really protecting me now?

4. What would help me better in this situation?

5 What is the usefulness of the system that I'm using, where is its place, and how can it be repurposed?

As we said when describing emotional states, there is no human reaction that does not have a function. Nothing is good or bad. It simply has to be the most appropriate, proportionate and efficient reaction to face each specific situation. If we have a hammer, it will be the most effective tool to drive a nail, but we can't saw a plank with it. If a protection system is disproportionate, out of place or the consequences are worse than doing nothing, we must change our automatic response and plan our reactions in a reflective way. To do this, it's necessary to go through a process of increasing awareness and having perspective. On this basis, we can begin to test different possibilities.

12 RECOVERING FLEXIBILITY AND MOBILITY

Trust only movement. Life happens at the level of events, not of words. Trust movement. Alfred Adler.

The village where the protagonists of the following story lived was destroyed some time ago by a fire which decimated the forest and their crops. Four of the villagers were left without a means to survive and were able just to get by, thanks to the aid of the Town Hall. One day a family with a little child passed through the village, and while the parents talked with the villagers, the child ran around, as children do. After some time, he appeared with four bags of seeds and twigs and gave one to each villager, telling them that they could then re-plant and grow crops again.

One of the villagers threw away the bag when he got home, thinking that there was no solution, because the child's fancy reminded him of his misfortune. The second one gave all the seeds to his bird, the only company that he had, and the only thing that he still cared about in this life. The third villager clung to the idea that seeds would be the solution and planted each one, carefully heavily watering them every day. The fourth one said to himself, "What have I got to lose?" and in his free time planted the seeds and watered them occasionally. At the same time, he sought out government aid, which he used to fix his house and replant the forest.

When spring came, some of the seeds had germinated in the third villager's garden, and especially in the fourth villager's. Envious of their luck, the first two looked at them and lamented their fate even more. Some of the plants grew into trees, but mostly they made the villagers feel hope at seeing grow something where before there had only been destruction. That changed their mood and helped their life return to normal. The third villager did not enjoy it very much, because despite the fact that things had gotten better, he still felt that he had not done enough and worked even harder to reach his increasingly higher expectations, always feeling anxious and worn out. Obviously, the fourth villager was the one who had made the most of a simple bag of seeds.

Extended traumatic experiences often leave us in an emotional state that is denominated learned helplessness[20]. When scientists give laboratory animals an electric shock when they go through the door that leads to food, they choose not to leave. Even when the shock no longer happens, they will never go through the door again. Similarly, in severely traumatized human beings, it's common that when later on they are in situations where a way out is available to them, and they have options, they don't know how to use them to their advantage. They give up without trying, assuming it won't work or that the cure is worse than the disease. The tendency to enact passive responses and not explore new alternatives is frequent. The repertoire of behaviors is limited, the person doesn't take risks, doesn't try out different possibilities and falls into a kind of resignation.

Spontaneity and creativity are the result of healthy development. Although we tend to think that both aspects are innate, and that naturally children have these characteristics, productive spontaneity and creativity can only occur in the context of a secure attachment that promotes safety and autonomy. Children that feel safe and protected can dare to explore their surroundings, be inventive and experiment. They occasionally return to the security of their caregiver and, once they have reconnected and feel safe, may venture out again with interest to explore the world around them. The caregiver will amplify their reactions of interest by sharing moments of playfulness and enjoyment, and will be protective in a proportional and consistent manner when necessary, so that the child doesn't have to deal with that part until they are able to do so themselves.

If our environment is hostile, we start using "damage control" mode. Our repertoire of behaviors becomes restricted, we always take the roads that we know best, and use systems that we feel that we have a command of. Being creative is a luxury that would require energy that we don't have. In the absence of a fluent mechanism for regulation, this energy is invested in scanning the environment to detect potential hazards and keeping our feelings under control.

This automatic functioning can be experienced as something beyond influence. We may become observers of our own actions, as if a part of ourselves was separate, while another one continues with life. There is no reflecting on whether this is beneficial for us or not, nor do we reflect on other alternatives. There is no decision-making, and there are no practical solutions. We just keep going on autopilot, as if everything had been scheduled at another time and in another place.

Change implies recovering manual control and exploring new alternatives. However, this presents the same difficulty as rehabilitating a muscle which has been tense and stiff for many years. Each stretch goes against the tendency of the body, and each set of exercises involves a certain amount of suffering while the function of each muscle group is recovered. In the earliest stages, it seems to cause more hard than good, and only after a patient works for months can they begin to enjoy the results.

What seems like a simple matter of a patient working to achieve results brings with it many difficulties in people who have gone through adverse interpersonal situations. By having lived through experiences that have caused us so much suffering, we can be determined not to feel that suffering anymore. Although the effort involved in working towards a healthy change is worthwhile, because over time it will ease our discomfort in a more solid and definitive manner, internally we can't distinguish one suffering from another, and we tell ourselves that it's not worth it. Furthermore, there will be times when we have to force ourselves to get up, when we'd rather just stay in bed all day, to go to therapy, to get things done or to interact with others even when we feel insecure. This way of "forcing ourselves" will act as a trigger for the memories for all the times we felt forced to do something we didn't want to do, and therefore we don't force ourselves to do them now (although it would help us). Finally, if the people surrounding us were unable to devote all the attention or affection that a child needs during childhood, whether because of personal limitations, disease or intentionality, it's likely that we will have internalized the same tendency to neglect our authentic needs or to not attend them. Although the need for affection still remains within us, we will ignore it or will behave in ways that end up enhancing the refusal or neglect of others. A pattern of appropriate self-care and a capacity to connect to and regulate our emotional states is lacking or dysfunctional, because the most significant models that surrounded us were not a healthy reference. For this reason, when we are finally able to make changes that would help us, we don't consider them to be a priority.

From this point of view, the process of overcoming our problems when we have lived in traumatizing environments involves helping ourselves to experiment. In the beginning, we have to do this in a "forced mode," since this does not often occur naturally. Just like when we start going to the gym, at the beginning we will notice that we are stiff or out of shape, and doing exercise will be hard. We will just barely be able to stretch, and when we push a little, our muscles will ache. The first weeks are full of soreness, and each class will wear us out. But if we persist, after a few months we really will start to feel better, tire less easily, and master the exercises. Recently acquired movements will become familiar, and we can try things that are more complicated.

No matter how bad we feel and how much we blame it on bad luck, if we keep doing the same old things, what is more likely is that we will continue to feel the same way. If after trying something 50 times we don't get the result that we want, the 51st attempt won't be successful either. However, human beings have an incredible ability to continue making the same mistakes or using the same tactics for dealing with a situation, because we tell ourselves that it's what we need to or must do, or that we are just that way, and it doesn't matter if our "solution" won't really work for that problem, even when we have tested its ineffectiveness many times. Any other options that we might think of would make more sense. For example, we can blame a person for treating us a certain way, but we see that the situation keeps repeating itself. So let's try something, but not the same way as always: let's try any other alternative and see what results it produces. If we keep trying different things, we will find better solutions, or least solutions that are not as bad as before. If it doesn't work, it doesn't matter, because making mistakes is the best way to learn. The important thing is to not make the same mistake over and over again. When we resolve to make these changes, it is important to realize that we may feel strange. The ideas that we will try to put into practice may seem absurd and illogical, but remember that appearance is not the most important thing, but rather the results, both in the medium and long term. Of course, our attempts must make sense with regards to our greatest difficulties. For example, if we have problems tolerating loneliness, we can do exercises on "scheduled alone time," such as doing little things by ourselves that we would usually do with someone else. People who do not feel comfortable being alone tend to avoid it unless there is no choice, but this way of functioning has major side effects. On one hand, when inevitably we find ourselves alone, we may feel that it's unbearable and do whatever - sometimes of little benefit to us - to avoid feeling lonely. On the other hand, relationships will become even more complex than they should be, since we put extra pressure on them to ensure that others will always be there. If we identify these difficulties, we can schedule some daily tasks to take care of by ourselves, reverse the process, and give ourselves an opportunity to get used to, normalize and even enjoy, the feeling of being alone. As a rule of thumb, the stranger a task feels, the better the direction we have taken. That means that we were stretching the stiffest muscle. We can, for example, go to the movies alone. If we think about it, it's an activity we don't actually need company for, because we are focused on the movie most of the time. We can go to a coffee shop or a restaurant alone, and look for different situations each day, all of them without the company of others. We don't try to escape from the feeling of loneliness, which initially may be uncomfortable, but try to feel it for a while. We will surely connect with moments from our past, perhaps early memories, when we felt isolated, abandoned or helpless, but the current situation is absolutely different. The adult that we are can understand how difficult it is for a child to feel unloved and unprotected, to experience that lack of support, but we can differentiate it very well from the positive aspects of being self-sufficient adults. Being alone is not negative in and of itself; in fact, it is a feeling which sometimes can be pleasant. For this purpose, we must unlink that sensation from our first or worst early feelings of loneliness and re-associate it with everyday situations without that negative meaning. Although we understand what it represented for us at that time, we remind ourselves that we are now in a completely different stage in life.

Another task, however strange it may sound, is to "adopt a sock." If we are slaves to control and need to keep everything in order, we need to put a sock in our life. We will put this balled up sock somewhere visible and very much out of place. If just the thought of this bothers us, this is definitely something we need to do. We will place our sock friend at home and not move it until - long after - we are no longer conscious of its presence. Meanwhile, as the days go by, we will look at it, observe it for a few minutes, and when we notice discomfort, we will remind ourselves that we are getting used to a sensation that will free us from our enslavement to control. Thus, when something happens - as it often does - and things go off course, we will be more capable of accepting it.

We can make these sensations more tolerable by introducing humor and creativity with more extravagant attempts. Even so, it's expected that some unpleasant emotions will arise, the same as when stretching a muscle, because it only works well when it's a bit uncomfortable. The key is to not plan impossible or overly-ambitious tasks which we abandon for months after having spent all our energy on them the first day.

These experiments are like the seeds in the tale of the villagers. The more we sow, the more possibilities we will reap later in the season. Results won't come immediately, because the seeds must germinate and then the plants need time to grow. If, like some of the villagers, we discard attempts because we think that they don't make sense or that they won't work, we are denying ourselves a chance. If we strive desperately to achieve positive, immediate results by putting pressure on ourselves, we will generate distress that depletes our energy and will make failure more likely. Each experiment counts, regardless of the outcome, because everything that is different from pathological automatic repetitions increases our flexibility.

Post-traumatic inflexibility requires stretching and push-ups, exercise charts and perseverance, the same as when we are physically stiff. If we have the internal belief that everything depends on fate and the elements, and that there is nothing we can do, we won't try anything, and consequently, we won't get anything. This is the same feeling that the mice in the learned helplessness experiment had, but the key difference is that we are not lab rats. We can get perspective on what is happening, understand what is going on, become aware of our feelings, and not be ruled by them. If we see with our capacity for reflection that there are many options available, even if our intuition pushes us to one side, in this case we won't follow it. We know that our intuition may have been programmed in another time to prevent situations that are no longer present or that have other conditioning factors.

13 ALLOWING MYSELF TO BE VULNERABLE AGAIN

It is madness to hate all roses because you got scratched by one thorn, to give up on your dreams because one did not come true. Antoine Saint-Exupery.

Let's think back on the cat and rabbit, and how they reacted when we rubbed their bellies. As we said, the cat lets us touch it and enjoys the pampering to its fullest, because it knows that it has claws and could use them before we can react. It's exposed, but at the same time, it feels protected. It may show its vulnerability to another individual, precisely because it knows that it can protect itself.

Regaining the capacity to experience our vulnerability as a resource for connecting with others allows us to have close relationships without fear and without being defensive. This is a huge challenge for all those who have been damaged in significant interpersonal situations, even more so if the danger was associated with our first experience of connection. If we later experience damage again with people we trust, we can ask ourselves if it is worth it to trust again. It seems logical to believe that if we don't establish deep relationships, we can protect ourselves from harm. On the contrary, this withdrawal from relationships is the greatest damage we can do to ourselves. And this time we are the ones who cause the damage.

Imagine that we are passionate about soccer but we have sustained an injury on the field. Once we recover, what should we do? If we never play soccer again, we will avoid getting hurt in the same way, but we will also quit doing something that we like a lot, forever depriving ourselves of the positive feelings that it brought us. Let's take another example: we love chocolate cake, but we choked on a piece of it, thought we were going to die and were very scared. To prevent this from happening again, will we give up our favorite dessert forever? Will we stop eating all together?

From a logical point of view, ceasing to do those things does not protect us, because whenever we walk, stumbling and falling is a possibility. Even if we stay home all day, we can trip over the rug. Maybe we decide not to go to the soccer field, but we end up walking into a lamppost. We might not choke on a piece of cake, but we do on a carrot. Not doing those actions is more of a magic trick than real protection, and it's not effective. The problem is that we accept our thoughts, "soccer is dangerous" or "chocolate cake is harmful," without questioning them.

These reactions, however, are frequent, even in the literal sense of the examples that we have set. Many people who have had a car accident no longer drive or who got sick eating oysters never eat them again. Those who overcome life's circumstances and deal with these situations within a short period of time are the ones who gradually regain security in themselves. If we avoid things that have damaged us by chance, but that are positive and harmless in and of themselves, we are going to limit ourselves unnecessarily.

Sometimes things are more complex because we never had the pleasant sensation of feeling vulnerable and quiet in the arms of someone who is not going to pressure or damage us, or because we never felt secure and protected in a relationship. If we grow up in a family with many problems, with caregivers who are ill or traumatized, or very chaotic and unpredictable, or if there are very serious bonding problems, being vulnerable can become synonymous with suffering severe damage. Coming from these circumstances, believing that being vulnerable is good and does not imply danger would require an act of faith, because all the evidence we have seems to go against it. However, deep inside all humans is a strong need for connection, which continues to influence our behavior whether we like it or not. Saying that we don't need bonds with other people is like saying that we don't need to breathe. Sometimes the air is toxic, but not breathing is not an option either.

The good news is that we can regain the ability to show our vulnerability to someone, and at the same time feel a sense of security. To do this, we need to heal our wounds and feel that we can protect ourselves. Of course, it's not so simple. Healing our wounds implies recognizing that they are there, and realizing that although we think "we're over it," there is still deep and unsettled pain linked to our memories. It's necessary for us to clean these wounds and let the air get to them. This often involves resorting to a professional who knows how to heal the wounds and minimize the pain. In order to feel like we can protect ourselves, we must learn to reevaluate the danger a situation might present for us, unlock our instinctive defensive reactions, dismantle our dysfunctional protection systems, and rehearse healthy responses over and over again until we master them and they become second nature.

Achieving this implies a process of change. But remember that trauma leads to rigidity, and in a rigid system, transformation does not usually occur spontaneously. It will require a continued effort, and it won't be easy because we don't have healthy references and are quite lost. Therefore, it can be necessary for us to engage in a therapeutic process that usually requires a long period of time, and which may include many ups and downs, until we get results. Here lies the second difficult issue. With an unhealthy way of taking care of ourselves, a tendency to distrust others, and difficulties with interpersonal connection, engaging in therapy will be very difficult for us. Many people who have experienced significant traumas suffer from the consequences for years without seeking help, or ruling it out immediately. They tell themselves that what happened to them was not so important, that it's over, and that they have to move forward, because they do not assign any weight to what they feel. Remember the mother who said "Come on, it's nothing, don't cry" to the child with the scraped knee? They survived by going forward and never looking back. They tell themselves to be strong and do everything on their own, because they never had any support or when they did have it, it was counterproductive; in any case they are so used to not asking anyone for help, that they believe it should always be this way. They may be afraid to stir up the past because they think that it will only make them feel pain, and it won't do them any good. It may be impossible for them to trust a therapist; they may find that each candidate has drawbacks, or feel misunderstood or poorly treated when faced with the slightest of disagreements. They may be so afraid of change or have such negative expectations for the future, that they reject any method before trying it because they are convinced that it won't help them. They can feel so much guilt that they may believe that they don't deserve to feel good, or are so afraid of being disappointed that they prefer to have zero expectations of getting out of this situation, just like the laboratory mice that do not go for the food, even though the door is open. They no longer try and give up before they even start.

When a person decides to initiate therapy, difficulties are still frequent. Let's remember that the main trauma comes from relationships, and psychotherapy is a process of change that stems from the bond between patient and therapist. Therapy is a kind of relationship in which the person has to expose their most vulnerable aspects to another human being and trust them. This is precisely the problem the person has sought help for, and paradoxically, has to overcome in order to be able to solve it. This gives rise to many complex situations throughout the therapeutic process which we should understand as logical in this situation. We must be patient with ourselves and give things the time they need.

It's also possible that, on the contrary, the person might embark on a counterproductive therapy that lasts years. They cling to this relationship, which is significant for them but that is not part of their real life, in the conviction that they are incapable of establishing a genuine bond on their own. They may use the therapist as a witness to how bad they feel, without moving in any direction to change their situation. It's possible for them to waste all their energy by challenging their therapist, objecting to all their suggestions without ever trying them out, transmitting the belief that "it's never enough," that they carry within, rejecting countless therapists because none are good enough or insisting that their case is "too serious or unsolvable." In all these cases, the internal conflict the patient lives in is transmitted to the therapeutic relationship, which provides the person a certain feeling of control, but at the same time, keeps them from productive objectives, and prevents them from regaining control over their own lives.

Apart from their involvement in therapy, people suffering from interpersonal trauma can fear intimacy in general. They often have difficulties making friends or keeping them, because they do not trust anyone or because they expect undying loyalty in return, and hope to get from them everything they were denied in childhood. If we don't forgive mistakes or if we expect something uncharacteristic of an adult relationship, such as absolute and unconditional dedication or limitless generosity, establishing emotional bonds will be extremely difficult. Furthermore, when a relationship becomes closer, alarms may start going off, since we suffered the greatest damage in our closest relationships. We can become hypersensitive to both rejection and distancing or the very sensation of having opened the doors can instinctively lead us to close them.

Intimate relationships are another difficult task, even more so than relationships among friends. With a partner, the attachment system is activated, bringing with it what we have learned in that area. All scenarios are possible: the reluctance towards having a partner; the self-sabotage of relationships, especially when they become closer and more intimate; the oscillation between overdependence and disproportionate reactions of protection; and the tendency to find extreme and dependent relationships. This last situation may lead people to do whatever the other wants, whether it is beneficial or harmful for them. Another possibility is that the constant demands for affection end up exhausting the other person, because the unmet emotional needs are from the past, and without working on those memories, no matter how much affection the other one gives, it will never be enough.

Finally, many people who have had a difficult childhood or traumatic experiences with partners reject the idea of having children. They feel unable to raise their potential children, because they are very aware of the damage that can be done to a child. Nevertheless, while it's true that the attachment style which we have grown up with may be reflected in the one that we have with our children, many people who have had difficulties in their childhood take good care of their children. The unavoidable issue is that our brain resorts to our childhood experiences as a reference to know what to do in our children's upbringing. This experience can be used as a positive example or as a sign of what we don't want to do. Not infrequently, by trying to differentiate ourselves from our caregivers, we tend to do the opposite of what they did, which is also a problem, because, as we know, extremes are never good. But if we are aware of our tendencies and their origins, and we work to change them, we can relate to our children differently; we can relate to them in our own way.

Being aware of our difficulties in relationships is essential to being able to modify them. Saying that in order to feel good, it is crucial to regain our capacity to feel vulnerable with other human beings and establish close bonds with our friends, our partner and our children does not, however, mean that we must minimize the complexity involved in restoring our system of connecting with others when it has been seriously damaged.

Looking at our problems honestly and realistically, and at the same time without blaming ourselves for having difficulties that we did not purposely choose and without resigning ourselves to continuing to be this way, will allow us to have life's most special experience, which comes from a deep connection with others. No matter how afraid we are of this idea, there is nothing that is more worthwhile. When we experience the healing of our wounds, we will also know that we can risk connecting with others because, even if we suffer again, the damage is never permanent. It's true that if we expose ourselves we can get hurt, but if our protection systems work optimally, the damage won't be extensive, nor will it take long to heal. By touching our scars, we know from experience that all pain eventually subsides. If we weigh up what we gain - which is greater now that we know how to connect with others better - and what we lose - which is less now that we take better care of ourselves and protect ourselves more - we will feel that it's worth the effort.

14 PUTTING RESPONSIBILITY IN ITS PLACE

The best years of your life are the ones in which you decide your problems are your own. You do not blame them on your mother, the ecology or the president. You realize that you control your own destiny. Albert Ellis.

One of the advantages of feeling that I'm not the one who does, thinks or feels certain things, is that I don't assume responsibility for these reactions. We can blame ourselves afterwards for having them and pay the consequences, but if we don't assume responsibility for changing them, our guilt is counterproductive. Our disturbance only feeds the cycle, because we feel so bad for having an explosion of rage, that we constantly torture ourselves internally, so our despair rises, and our mood drops. This emotional state leads to a cumulative discomfort, which ends up causing a new outburst.

Sometimes we use this lack of control over our reactions as an excuse to minimize the consequences of our actions. We tell others that we did not mean what we said or ask them to take us at our word, because they know what our temper is like. Our intentions are good, but "we can't avoid" having these outbursts. While it's true that these reactions are still not integrated and under our conscious control, it's also true that it's up to us to work on making changes. The things we do or say, even impulsively and without premeditation, have consequences that are our responsibility. This does not mean that we have to torture ourselves for having done it; not only does this not fix the problem, but in fact it can make things worse. The real responsibility is accepting the problem and fixing it. If we can't do it alone, as it would be expected, we should seek out help, and no matter how hard, let others help us.

Taking responsibility means getting along better with our sense of guilt. Culpability involves suffering when it is disproportionate, when we are loaded down with guilt that isn't ours. When guilt is fair, when we feel it because we really made a mistake, it's in its place. It's as if our boss respectfully points out that we have done our job poorly. If we see that he is right, we simply try to improve. Without guilt, we wouldn't care about how we do things and would continue making mistakes.

Some children grow up in families where adults never take responsibility for their actions, never acknowledge that they are wrong, or never accept guilt for anything. This culpability that floats in the air is often taken on by the children, who usually tend to relate everything that happens to themselves. Furthermore, if someone explicitly blamed them, this tendency will increase. When they become adults, they may keep on bearing the responsibility for the behavior of others. If they have a very critical partner who accuses them constantly, they assume that they are guilty without questioning it.

These family contexts, both in childhood or in partner relationships, are not necessarily related to violence. Living with a person who is overly convinced of always being right, who expresses his opinions in a conclusive and unappealable manner, makes those around him more insecure and prone to questioning themselves. Authoritarian, critical, demanding or perfectionist personalities may produce similar effects. In any case, others must take the blame when something is different from how they want it to be.

As explained above, extreme situations in the family context also lead to extreme mechanisms of adaptation. On one hand, we can assume guilt for something we did not do and constantly blame ourselves. But on the other hand, we may refuse to take responsibility for solving our problems or refuse to go to therapy to change them, saying that we don't need anybody, that we don't want to talk about our issues with other people, or that what has happened has no solution. Both extremes may coexist, and even if we constantly complain about feeling bad, we do nothing to change.

If we have developed patterns of functioning that are negative both for us and for others, and they have not changed or have been getting even worse with time, it's clear that we have to do something to change them. What does not make sense is to keep doing everything the same way, with the expectation that the situation will evolve positively.

What we tell ourselves can give us multiple excuses and reasons to keep going down the same path. We can tell ourselves that we are not able to change, that we don't have the strength, that our circumstances leave us no choice, or that we have tried everything and that others have to change. The list of excuses goes on and on, and when we say them to ourselves, we experience them as if they were unquestionable truths. One of the first changes that we need to address is to modify these statements. Instead of, "I'm not able to" we might say, "It's hard for me." Instead of, "I can't" we may say, "I don't want to." If this last statement gives us reason to doubt, we might consider, for example, when we don't leave home to go for a walk because "we can't," but on other occasions we take the dog for a walk, deliver a document that is due that day, or go to a doctor's appointment. If we can do those things, we can also wake up at a specific time in the morning to get back into a daily routine or go to the park near our house so as not to be stuck at home all day. Maybe we can't do all that much if we are feeling quite down, but what we do with the little energy we have left is our decision. If we start to assume our own responsibility, we won't allow ourselves to say flat out "I can't." In the event that we decide not to do something, we will say, "I didn't do it because I chose not to."

Another way of not taking responsibility is by letting ourselves get caught up in complaints. If we complain a lot, even when we only do so internally, we are stuck in a trap for sure. We can always find a reason to complain if we look for one carefully, even when things are going well. We do this just by picking out the worst moments of the day, the people who treated us the worst, the details about others that we like the least, or the most terrible parts of our past, and letting our mind ruminate on these. When we look at the negative aspects of everything, we don't focus on our role in these issues or on what we do with them. Additionally, we place ourselves - again - in a position of helplessness instead of focusing on the development of our resources to deal with these situations. This is a counterproductive complaint that generates feelings of misunderstanding, abuse, and bitterness, but that does not change any of these situations. Curiously, underneath this attitude may be intense guilt which we can't tolerate and which we may be unaware of. So, we project culpability and blame others or the world in general, for all our problems. The issue is if 100% of the problem is outside us, we also put the solutions beyond our reach. Even in those stages of life when problems that were difficult to solve seemed to happen all at the same time, time spent complaining is often wasted time. Of course, it's good to be able to let off steam from time to time, and it's not always more productive to put on a good face. Remember: both extremes tend to be equally negative.

Failure to take responsibility can also come from a stagnation in our childhood pattern. We felt helpless as a child, or we did not know how to protect ourselves from a harmful relationship with our partner, we can remain in that emotional state and think that, since we feel helpless and unprotected, we actually are. As we had no options in the original situations, we don't make decisions in the present ones, assuming that everything remains the same. If we make an unsuccessful attempt, right after something goes wrong, we give up, confirming our theory that there is nothing we can do. It's as if we are still small, helpless and unable to stand up for ourselves. And while this was true in the early stages of our life, when we become adults, things are very different. Expecting someone to come and rescue us from ourselves usually does not work. When we put our hope in others, such as friends, partners or children who we take care of, to protect us or save us from our fate, what we are doing doesn't fit with our stage in life. We operate like children when we no longer are, and this pattern we are in corresponds to another developmental time and does not fit our present situation.

As explained above, as we grow up, we internalize the models of regulation and care from those around us, and as a result, develop systems of self-care and self-regulation. In adulthood, what comes from the outside always passes through an internal filter. If we don't regulate our emotions, if we neglect ourselves, if we self-criticize too harshly, get angry with ourselves, or simply do nothing to regulate our emotions, positive attitudes from others won't reach us deep inside. Being cared for by others can satisfy our needs only if our system is structured toward self-care. A reassuring gesture or consoling words can't neutralize the negative effect that comes from putting pressure on ourselves or blaming ourselves for feeling bad. If we do nothing when our emotions run unchecked, other people will fail to calm us, because - unlike what happens with babies - others do not have direct access to our internal regulatory system. If our rage is geared inward, although we find a protective figure, we are causing ourselves more damage. We are the only ones who have the key to our inner world and have to actively participate in its reconfiguration. On top of our self-regulation, we can benefit from external resources, which can heighten - but never replace - the way in which we manage our emotional states.

There is no chance of recovery without taking personal responsibility to achieve it. Improvement won't come from a pill that fixes everything, a person who gives us what we lacked, a job that gives us the motivation that we didn't have or something unexpected that rescues us from ourselves. Leaving our future to chance is pointless. It's important to strive to make it possible, but without turning the fight against ourselves.

If we think about it, taking on this responsibility is, in and of itself, refreshing. It means that we can take control of our life, no matter how difficult the road becomes. We are no longer in the hands of others, nor do we want to be; we are in control of our life. It's normal to be afraid of this, because as much as we understand that making mistakes is part of the process, taking responsibility for our bets and decisions means that they can go wrong. When others are the perpetrators, or if we consider fate as the root of our problems, there is no possibility to fail. However, making this change can be difficult for us. When we already carry around a heavy burden of guilt that is not a result of our own actions, it feels as if just one additional responsibility will do us in.

Let's remember here that guilt is our friend. We are not talking about unfair and misplaced blame, but the guilt that is proportional to our mistakes, which helps us to improve, to try again and to do it in a more realistic and efficient way. Change is not possible if we don't follow down-to-earth parameters and have a healthy sense of guilt that gets activated when we do something wrong in our own eyes or in the eyes of others. This helps us from falling into self-indulgence and irresponsible behavior. We need to look at our problems without torturing ourselves over them and say, "I have to do something about it." It's essential that, in addition to saying it, the feeling moves us towards action. It does not matter if our attempts are effective or not, because as we know, many trials are needed before getting a result.

15 MY ADULT SELF DRIVES THE CAR

We are what we do, especially what we do to change what we are.
Eduardo Galeano.

We may be tethered to many feelings and sensations from our childhood or from a difficult experience, and it's possible that, as adults, we have stuck to certain beliefs about ourselves and the world. When things happen in our first years of life, our ability to influence their outcome is very limited. We were conditioned to believe that those who raised us would realize what was happening to us and take steps to remedy it. If they did not realize what was happening or chose not to do anything about it, we had no choice. But we are adults now, and as adults, we always have options.

It's very likely that we don't see what those options are. Sometimes, this is because we think that they are not plausible. We try to solve our problems by imagining that we have moved to a deserted island where no one bothers us. The thing is, we are not millionaires, and we don't have an island to go to, and when we realize this, we fall further into despair. We don't consider small, practical solutions which are possible in the medium and long term and which really bring about change.

At other times, although the options are there, and we can see them, we operate within a sense of helplessness, not being able to do anything by ourselves and being trapped in situations. Those feelings were absolutely real in childhood, but we don't realize that in the here and now, things are not the same. Although we continue to live with our birth family, we are no longer children, but adults. Although we remain in the same problematic relationship, we don't have to sit and wait for everything to change without doing anything. If we are aware that we are adults and we are in the driver's seat, our perspective takes a radical turn. We know that solving our problems depends on us, so we must take the reins and assume our responsibility.

This last sentence may generate discomfort for us when reading it, but it's essential for moving forward. Perhaps we are reading this and thinking, "It's not fair - how can it depend on me? The other people are the ones who should treat me better. How can I be okay if my parents, my husband, my boss, or my children all treat me this way?" And the answer is yes, we can be better although they all remain the same. Luckily, in every relationship, we can always modify our 50%. That gives us sufficient margin to move things.

We might think, "But how? My mother still treats me like a child." And that is where we must remind ourselves that we are now adults; despite the fact they treat us like children, we are not. If we don't let the child who was left locked inside us talk to our mother, but instead allow the adult to have the conversation, even though we are aware that there are many childhood feelings still there, that conversation is going to turn out very differently from how it usually does. Over time, if we work on our past, and we resolve the feelings that are still active from that stage, that discomfort will no longer be in the background, and we will feel completely different. But the change starts beforehand. It begins when we cease to be in the passenger seat, waiting for someone to come and drive us far away from where we are now.

Sometimes, when we endure adverse situations for a long time, we dream of a rescuer who ends it or a genie in a bottle who grants us three wishes. We may fantasize about someone discovering that we are not really a member of this family and that our real parents suddenly appear, or that we move to another country. The imaginary solution to our problems would be one day to find love that gives us everything that we have been denied, to have children who give us everything we missed out on or to reach our dreams in life. Fantasizing is an escape, and above all during childhood, fantasy is a powerful resource that allows us to disconnect from things that we can't change. However, we can stay stuck in that position, waiting for something to rescue us from ourselves, even when there are things we can do to change.

Certainly, the real solutions won't come as a result of the dramatic shift that we have imagined - we won't wake up one morning and find that everything is different. But we can do something, something concrete, perhaps small, but real. Thousands of small changes move the world. To do this, we must modify our perspective.

The first change is to realize that we are adults, that we make our own decisions, that we are in the driver's seat. The second is to be clear about what which road we should take. When the important figures in our lives haven't taken care of us in a healthy way, it can be easy to replicate those same patterns internally by blaming, being demanding of or even abandoning ourselves. A way of identifying these patterns is by examining our list of priorities. Logically, if we feel bad, our priority should be to feel better. If we don't feel good, it will be very difficult to manage everything else. However, looking for things that are beneficial for us can be very low on our list, and instead, we prioritize what we need to do, what others need, and what is expected of us. Of course, sometimes we must fulfill a certain number of responsibilities, and caring about others is good and functional. What doesn't make sense is to always put what is good for us in last place, and even less if we don't feel good and want to feel better. What is good for us should come first, especially when we feel bad and our emotional batteries are drained, and this means giving other items on the list lower priority.

Sometimes what is good for us is not even on the list. We may think that if we seek things that are good for us, this means that we are selfish, and completely throw that idea out. Perhaps deep down we feel we don't deserve good things or that we will never be able to have them. An even worse, although quite common, version is that even when by chance good things happen, we neutralize them, push them away or sabotage them. How can we feel okay if we don't look for things that are beneficial to us or if when they do happen, we don't allow ourselves to feel them?

Therefore, change starts when we modify the question. We say to ourselves, "I don't feel like going out today, but… will it be good for me?" And we don't cheat; we take our time before responding, and we stop to reflect on how we felt when we got home at the end of the day after taking a long walk, compared to the days when we stayed in bed, with the curtains drawn, thinking about the same things over and over again. Whether we feel like it or not is something we should consider, but it matters more if that something is beneficial to us or not. When we are feeling down or overwhelmed, doing what our body asks does not necessarily improve our situation.

Nevertheless, just doing things for the sake of it is not the solution. When someone is depressed, those around them often tell them to cheer up, to do their part and try to function normally. Based on this line of reasoning, behaving as if we feel good should make us feel good. These suggestions are in the same vein as the mother who reacted to the scraped knee with: "Come on, don't cry, it doesn't matter." As we saw, this is not the best way to manage emotions. Sometimes the best thing we can do for ourselves is precisely not to do certain things. In that case, we don't leave our home to please others, doing what they expect us to do or because we are supposed to, but instead we stay at home because it's better for us to rest. We know that this is true because we have seen that when we force ourselves to do things at the same level as when we felt fine, we end up being exhausted at the end of day, and feel even worse the next morning. Considering this information, not doing that activity is the best thing we can do to help ourselves.

The question of whether something is good for us or not is applicable not only to external activities, but also to what we say to ourselves. The latter, although it's not visible, is even more important. Our mind is never quiet, but sometimes we are not aware of the constant dialogue with ourselves. We are constantly talking to ourselves about what we are doing, what we are thinking or how we feel. This internal dialogue is very important in the regulation of our emotions, and can work - as we explained above - either as an attenuator and modulator of our emotional states or as a sounding board that multiplies its intensity. Becoming aware of this internal dialogue and introducing changes in it is one of the bases of the work we have to do in order to get better. We must switch from automatic to manual and help our minds to turn from what we tend to say, towards telling ourselves the things that help us more.

For this change to happen, we should re-train our mind. It's essential to understand where the problem lies, but it's only the first step. We must consider this to be an exercise program that we have to repeat regularly, until the new way of talking to ourselves is so internalized that it comes to us naturally. For a time, we must pay more attention to this and stay on top of this training to make sure it is maintained and consolidated.

This set of mental exercises consists of a sequence of questions. We must always ask ourselves the questions in this order, and even though we know the answer, we must ask the question and answer it every single time. If we go through these questions over and over again, we will be redirecting our mind towards another way of functioning, seeing and understanding ourselves, as well as taking care of ourselves internally. The power this change has on improving our well-being is huge, although we may notice it only after a time. Now let's look at these questions.

What do I say to myself?

Our thoughts can go unnoticed if we don't pay attention to them. When we feel bad, we may think that there are no thoughts or that there is only distress, but thoughts are always there. We are usually telling ourselves something about what we are experiencing. We may think, for example, "I can't stand feeling like this," "I'm an idiot for allowing this to happen," "It's all my fault," "I'll never get out of this" or "I wish I were dead." In any of these examples, these phrases are not simple consequences of our emotional distress, but will generate new negative sensations within us or worsen the ones that we already have. It may help to write these phrases down, word for word, as we are saying them to ourselves. Seeing them on paper can make us more aware of the number of insults that we say to ourselves or to what extent we discourage or discredit ourselves internally.

Where did I learn this?

Very often these phrases recreate things we heard from significant figures in our lives. Our parents, teachers or partners may have said, "You're unbearable," "You're an idiot," "It's all your fault," "You're unfixable," or "You never should have been born." This is not always the case, but often the way in which we talk to ourselves internally mirrors how important figures from our past talked to us. We see ourselves as others saw us, treat ourselves as we were treated. The issue is that once we internalize that model, we carry it with us. We can be far away from these people, or they may no longer be part of our life, but their influence is still there. The problem is that we can't get away from ourselves, although we try to do it in a thousand ways. Our head is on our shoulders 24 hours a day. We have no choice but to reprogram our mind.

Did it help me when those people said it to me?

Although it's obvious that no one likes other people telling us that we are unbearable, a mess, guilty or good for nothing, It's essential to be aware of how bad these statements made us feel and that they were unhelpful and stirred up uncomfortable sensations in us from the very beginning. This was the air that we breathed in those relationships, and if we stop to think about it, we surely will consider this to be a legacy that we don't want to hold on to.

Would it help me if the people who are around me now said the same things?

If we relate to different people now, let's imagine that they say "You won't be able to handle this", "You're an idiot for feeling this way," "It's your fault that you're in this situation," "You aren't going to improve" or "You'd be better off dead." How would we feel if we heard this? Again, it's obvious that that we'd feel bad, but let's ask ourselves the question and answer it anyway. It can help us become aware of what it means to us when we do the same internally and often continuously. Therefore, sometimes not seeing anyone or staying at home doesn't help us rest, as we can be our own worst enemy.

Would I say that to a loved one that matters to me?

Let's imagine ourselves doing this. Think of our best friend, our children or a loved one. Suppose they are feeling exactly like we are, and then we say to them, "You won't be able to handle this," "You're an idiot for feeling this way," "It's your fault, that you're in this situation," "You aren't going to improve," or "You'd be better off dead." Surely it seems aberrant and unthinkable to do so. It's important to become aware of the terrible things that we can come to tell ourselves. Although we still have not changed anything, if every time we said those things to ourselves, we realized that we were doing it, it would be like when a bad word gets bleeped out on TV; they no longer go unnoticed and won't float around in our head indefinitely. That reduces the problem and is already a significant change.

What would be helpful to say to myself?

Remember, if we are working on improving our emotional state, searching for what is good for us has to be the first thing on our list of priorities. Things that would help us are similar to those that help anyone else, so if we think what we would say to a loved one, we already have the answer. We can also think of what someone would say to us that would help us. For example, it would be good to tell ourselves that we will be able to deal with this, that it can happen to anyone, that we did what we could do; we could tell ourselves that with time, everything passes, that it will be hard, but we can move forward, that we are important, and that we deserve to feel good.

It's very possible that we don't believe ourselves when saying this, but the question of whether or not we feel it's true should not come first on our list. If a friend of ours is feeling bad because they are overweight, we don't say, "You're fat!" It may be somewhat true, but it won't help them at all to hear these kinds of things. Similarly, by reminding ourselves over and over again of the mistakes we have made or how bad we feel, we are just doubling down on our feelings of malaise. It's equivalent to falling into a hole and then digging to make it deeper. If we want to get better, it's important to learn to say to ourselves things that actually make us feel better. It doesn't matter if we believe it or not, or if it sounds weird. It's normal for it to be like this. If we have spent our life crushing ourselves internally, it will feel strange to treat ourselves right; in fact, it will feel almost alien. But if we keep repeating the new model of internal dialogue, it will end up sounding more natural. In a way it's like learning a new language. First, we repeat the words mechanically, saying the same phrases again and again, until our brain begins to assimilate and remember them. We won't be fluent in that language for a long time, but this is the normal learning process.

Our emotional states sometimes overwhelm us, flooding everything. We let our despair, discouragement and anguish make our decisions. We allow very old beliefs to continue to be our points of reference for our understanding of the world. But emotions do not think; they are actually like babies, like young children who simply feel, and we have to regulate, calm and encourage them in order for them to feel okay. It's very important to stay in touch with our emotions but at the same time, it's essential not to let ourselves be carried away by them. When we have many feelings accumulated inside, we can end up feeling like we did the moment we experienced them for the first time. We function like we aren't our real age, like defenseless, helpless, angry or spoiled children who have been left to their own devices. We must pay close attention to these children, but this never means that we let a child drive the car. The adult who is inside us must learn, sometimes from scratch, to take care of our feelings, to understand our emotions and to be aware of our needs. When a healthy adult cares for a child, they perceive if the child's discomfort has to do with being hungry, sleepy or sick, and gives them what they really need and what is good for them. Although this learning did not happen earlier, we can learn it now. The adult we are now must be in charge of the process of change. We don't need to know how to do it - we just have to try. It's true that in order to learn to drive, someone has to teach us, or we have to go to a driving school. We don't need to teach ourselves when it's easier to learn from others. We may acquire the knowledge that we lack, and practice everything we need to develop skills that we did not have previously. But it's essential that we get in the car, take the wheel, and take control of our lives.

16 THE ONE WHO MAKES THE MOST MISTAKES IS THE ONE WHO WINS

A person who never made a mistake never tried anything new.
Albert Einstein.

Destin Sandlin is an engineer, and his colleagues built him a "backwards" bicycle which was engineered to turn the front tire in the opposite direction from the handlebars, so that every time the rider turned the handles left, the front tire went right - and the other way around[21]. When turned to the right, the bike would go to the left, and vice versa. Although the change that we need to make to ride this bike is simple, it's impossible to do it if we know how to ride a normal bike. However, Destin got it. He set it as a goal for himself, and then worked tirelessly to achieve it. He got on the bike every day, for eight months, until he began to get it right. He fell off many times during the process, but instead of giving up, he tolerated the feeling of failure and just tried harder and harder.

Whenever he got back on the bike, he noticed the hold that old patterns had on him. Every time he had ridden a conventional bike in his life, his brain developed neural connections, and these networks of connections had created the memory of how to ride a bike. His mind automatically went towards this procedural memory, even though, at a conscious level, he knew what had to be done to ride the bike backwards. Becoming aware of what we have to change will not make the changes happen by themselves, but it is an essential first step. After this step, many others must come, and we should go through them in the right order.

Getting to where we want to go, when deeply ingrained patterns lead us in another direction, requires a combination of sustained effort and going against ourselves a little. Striving and going against ourselves are not necessarily good or bad - it all depends on what our goal is. If we only strive to fulfill our duties or to please others, that effort just takes energy away from us and ends up wearing us out. If we do the opposite and ignore our real needs or what's important to us, we will only do ourselves harm. If, on the other hand, we work hard to improve, and we go against our negative or self-destructive tendencies, the effort will be worth it.

Another important aspect of our change is the positive assessment of our mistakes. If we had a teacher who humilitated or punished us whenever we did something wrong, it's likely that we had problems in that subject. Those who did well in the subject are those who thrived in the face of adversity, those who rose to a challenge to overcome a particular obstacle. The more difficult the subject was, the harder they tried. Alternatively, if we internalized what the teacher said and did, we may have ended up berating ourselves and getting completely blocked. It has been proved that, in the educational system, positive reinforcement works better than negative reinforcement. When we mess up, if we remind ourselves of all the things that we do well, we will greatly improve how we carry out the task at hand. Scolding someone for making mistakes, especially when it is intense, demeaning or continuous, will most likely result in blockage and negatively affect their performance. The way we react regarding our mistakes is important in learning how to change the pattern. Learning is achieved through trial and error, and error is an essential part. Without error, learning is not possible.

Let's reflect on how we learned to walk. As babies, did we just stand up one day and start walking confidently? No. We fell over, grabbed on to something, stumbled, caught hold of something, and stumbled again. In each one of those failed attempts, our nervous system learned something. In the beginning, we could only take a couple of steps, but the excitement on the faces of the adults around us encouraged us to keep trying. If we were called useless for taking only a few steps, it would not be very motivating. The same goes for every new ability acquired in childhood. We learn how to make a tower of blocks only after many failed attempts to make the parts fit, because we still don't know how to figure it out, and don't manage to get it right. Our nervous system is learning, and it does so with each and every mistake. After making many mistakes, we start to put the pieces together in the right way, and the tower stands on its own.

The villager who planted the most seeds was the one who harvested the most. While some seeds sprouted and grew, there were many others that did not germinate. We know that we are moving forward when our day is full of mistakes. This means that we are working on changing, that we are learning. It's clear that in order to have this new perspective, one must be fond of making mistakes.

How can we do this? It's quite simple: everything we practice is learned. If the simple idea of making a mistake becomes intolerable to us, we need to start doing a specific task: making mistakes on purpose, in a premeditated, deliberate way. Anyone that feels bad about every failure will probably argue against this idea by saying, "I already make enough mistakes every day," but this task only works if the mistakes are intentional. With things that we could do well, we voluntarily choose to do them wrong to increase our mental flexibility. Every day we try to do something wrong. They can be insignificant, harmless, meaningless errors, like not putting a period at the end of a sentence, arriving five minutes late, leaving a wrinkle when making the bed or wearing socks that don't match. The point is that every day we get on the bike and try to ride it, wobbling and falling off. The number of times we fall today is an indicator of the energy we have invested in improvement. After some time, making these mistakes will have a more positive meaning, and sometimes we can even have some fun with them. But to get there, we must first get used to the discomfort that is commonly associated with mistakes. The nervous system can grow accustomed to all kinds of sensations, if we experience them on a regular basis. The first time we drive a car we feel insecure and tense, but if we drive every day, it becomes more automatic and, once it's mastered, it can even become a relaxing activity. For this process of habituation to happen, it's important not to distract our minds from the feeling we want to get used to. If we feel bad about being late or making things worse on purpose, let's take note of that feeling. We will get used to it and it will no longer be there, if we repeat the process enough.

Many attempts to change things do not work because they are not continuous and persistent. If we try to ride Destin's bike, and whenever we fall, we say, "It's impossible, I'll never get it," and then we don't try again for a month, the change will take much longer or won't happen at all.

An important moment in Destin's adventure with his modified bike was that, after eight months of daily practice, he began to feel that he could handle it. He no longer needed to pay constant attention to riding it, and his body no longer pulled it in the opposite direction all the time. His movement and balance were much more smoother. The new connections formed in his brain began to prevail over the old ones. However, the slightest distraction caused him to lose his balance. His learning was still fragile, the new connections were not yet strong and solid enough. He had to spend a lot more time training until the new system of functioning was consolidated.

When learning healthier patterns of self-care and self-regulation, a similar process takes place. When trying to improve, if something unforeseen annoys or baffles us, it's all too easy to return to old patterns. We may feel that we have taken a step backwards but, on the contrary, it really means that we are moving forward. It's a crucial moment and it's essential that we get back on the bike immediately. These ruts are inevitable, but we can make them smoother and less intense if we resume our initial idea and start to practice as soon as possible. Above all, it's important not to dig the hole deeper. When we fall, if we blame ourselves for being this way again and tell ourselves that we are useless, that we won't ever achieve our goals, that it's useless, the hole will only get bigger, and it will be that much harder for us to climb out of it.

Even though we may be able to ride our bike confidently, let's not forget that the older connections have not left our brain - they have only receded into the background. After all this process, Destin tried to ride his normal bike again, and although for a few hours he couldn't, shortly thereafter, his brain regained access to the old circuits and he was able to ride just like before. In our life, when circumstances push us towards old patterns, it's relatively easy to return to them. For example, if we have a new partner who criticizes us excessively, like our parents did, we can begin to doubt and criticize ourselves internally again. We should always be attentive and never let our guard down.

But, if we work on it, most of the time that we spend taking care of ourselves will become natural and will occur spontaneously.

Self-regulation patterns can be relearned, as we have seen, but in the early stages of development, they emerge easily. It took two weeks for Destin's little boy to learn to ride the modified bike, the same process that took his father eight months of constant practice. Therefore, in order to understand things that happen to us as adults, it's good for us to explore if they have roots in our childhood. In our early experiences it's possible that we internalized messages or functioning styles, which then have continued to influence our perspective throughout the rest of our life. These situations may be evident or go unnoticed if we don't stop to reflect on them carefully. For example, growing up with a parent who is admired by everyone, who does everything perfectly, and who always has the right words and solution for every problem, can produce a more negative than positive effect in children. Faced with such a parent, the child thinks that they are not at their parent's level - nor will they ever be - and tends to feel insecure, defective or inadequate. The parent as a point of reference will mark the child's ideal of how they ought to be, but does not help them identify who they really are. This child will have difficulty tolerating their mistakes, and it's possible for them to feel like a failure, no matter how much they achieve. A parent who can never be questioned or one who doesn't seem to have any normal human flaws can become profoundly idealized but just like anyone else, they often have their high and lows. These figures may be people who rarely recognize their own mistakes, who easily point out the failure of others, who believe they are always right or do not empathize with others. Taking these parents off their pedestal may be difficult, but important. This will allow us to reconcile and value our own strengths and weaknesses. If we aren't people who grow from our mistakes, we should understand where this way of functioning comes from, because that can help us gain perspective.

We can change the way we are as well as the way we act in the world. This does not, however, happen like it does in the movies, after a sudden revelation. It's important for us to be realistic about the way things can be changed: through many mistakes. The one who is more often wrong is the one who has the highest chances of success.

17 QUESTIONING OUR BELIEFS: THE EVIL FROM GOOD AND THE GOOD FROM EVIL

Our most rooted and unquestioned convictions are those most open to suspicion. They are our limits, our confines, our prison. José Ortega y Gasset.

The evil from good

When we grow up in an upside-down world, sometimes words take on different or even contradictory meanings. In the world of dysfunctional attachment, care gets mixed up with worry, protection with control, and affection with obedience. If our emotional needs are not addressed, we can perceive these needs as something negative that we must ignore or suppress. If others punish us when we show an emotion, we can believe that this emotion is bad. Maybe the rules of this relationship game are contradictory or even absurd, but they are the only references we have to operate with. When we are in a chaotic or ambivalent environment, we don't know what to do to adapt, so we may end up clinging to any idea that can guide our behavior, and we probably won't stop to analyze whether it makes sense or not.

Often enough, our environment can contribute to that confusion. If we were told in early childhood that the color red was called green, and vice versa, when we say that something is green, we would mean red. In this way, we may come to the understanding that expressing our discomfort is the same as being weak, that having needs is equivalent to being selfish, that searching for affection is childish, and that being angry equates to being temperamental, fussy, spoiled or evil, because people around us give us those kinds of messages every time they see us in these emotional states.

But just because someone tells us something in a loud and resounding voice, someone who appears to be secure, it doesn't mean that they possess the absolute truth. In fact, when someone says something as if it were unquestionable, it's precisely for that reason that it's usually false. Conviction is very different from a healthy level of confidence. Healthy confidence allows room for doubt and lets us change our mind if someone puts forward reasonable arguments. In principle, conviction is always pathological and indicates a significant underlying need to cling to an idea. If someone were to call a sad child a crybaby, this adult most likely does not know what to do with their own sadness. If they were to tell the child that they were bad when the child was angry, they are probably incapable of managing their own stress. In all likelihood, the emotions that we show in those moments are uncomfortable for some people around us, because they also have their own difficulties handling them. Important figures that we grow up with can't teach us an emotional language that they themselves have not learned, and often they are trapped in their own counterproductive automatic patterns. They tell us these things, not because they are true, but just because of their own limitations. With those comments, they may also try to exert some degree of control over us or punish our behavior because they feel challenged by it or don't know how to deal with it. This doesn't mean that we have to make excuses for the behavior of people who may have caused us harm, but we should understand that their statements are just opinions which come from their own mental processes, and it's quite likely that they are very distorted.

Given that our internal dialogue mirrors the style of the important figures in our life, it's important for us to be open to questioning all our convictions. Many thoughts run through our mind without us ever stopping to analyze their logic. We think that just because we believe them so resolutely, they are absolutely and unquestionably true. It is precisely because we think these thoughts with such conviction that is highly likely that they are not.

However, if we have grown up in a complex, chaotic or ambivalent environment, the few points of reference that do we have about what we must do will seem to be absolutely essential and necessary. Without these references, we think that everything will turn into total chaos, and thus we cling to them. These ideas are the foundation of our perspective about ourselves and the world. We say that bad things happen to us because we are worth nothing, because everything is our fault, or because there is an adverse fate that determines our future. We not only tell ourselves this, but we cling to this idea, because at least this way things have an explanation. That way we can oddly resist modifying the negative belief that we are useless, and when other people remind us of our achievements, we underestimate what they say to us. Whenever they say something positive about us, we "smash" the comment with our mental bat and refuse to let it in. And conversely, when something goes wrong, we open the door and let that fact or the criticism from others reach us inside and resonate with our belief. Thus, the feeling of "I am useless" grows within us, immune to the evidence around us that there are things that we do well and people who value us.

Therefore, in order to change, we must be willing to break down the frameworks on which our perspectives are built, to question our beliefs completely, and to make sure that no matter how strongly we think those things, they are not absolute truths. Most likely, they are simple lessons that we learned and stored when our brain, like Destin's son's, was still very malleable and absorbed everything. When our beliefs become weak, we can feel uneasy and distressed, and even dizzy, and those uncomfortable sensations indicate that we are on the right track. We are going away from the false security of our convictions, and in this way, we can change our perspective.

As it's probably difficult for us to have an objective point of reference, it's important for us to pinpoint healthy figures that we know as a point of reference, or let ourselves be advised by people such as really close friends, therapists, and so on, who can understand our problem. We must become observers of the world and of people, as if we were explorers moving through reality and looking at it for the first time. How do people who function in a healthy way describe themselves? What do they say when they feel good? What do they say when they feel bad? If we want to feel good, it makes sense for us to use those people who we think function well as a point of reference. But as we know, when we ride a bicycle with the handlebars on backwards, logic also tends to be inverted. So, if we look at other people who appear to feel okay, we may find ourselves using that information as a point of comparison and scolding ourselves for not being like them, instead of using their model as something valuable to learn from. It's also easy for us to filter what we see through the lens of our previous beliefs and tell ourselves that we are worth nothing, and that we can't be like these people because we are intrinsically defective. When others tell us that we do have a great deal of value, we dismiss their comments, by telling ourselves that they only said that to encourage us, but deep down, that's not what they think. Our mind may distort reality in many ways, because it's terrified of letting go of our nuclear beliefs. If we lose the only things that we are sure about, what are we left with? What comes next? We might feel that it's preferable to have a negative reference than to have nothing at all.

In this upside-down world, what's good appears to be bad and what's bad appears to be good. Clinging to our ideas seems to give us keys to understanding ourselves and the world, but we don't really understand anything. We may think that only control can give us security, but it's a prison that does not allow us to make changes. We firmly believe that the solution is to isolate ourselves from others, but by doing so, we cause ourselves further emotional damage and leave ourselves without any emotionally nutritive experiences. Perhaps we cling to a harmful relationship, believing that we can't ever have anything better, and justify the suffering in our relationship because we love that person, as if affection is the only thing to care about. Let's remember, the essential question is not whether our feelings are true or not, but if that relationship is good for us or not.

We can imagine a partner who will love us more than anything in the world, and this apparently beautiful idea does not really let us live with our partner as they are, a person who, logically, has flaws. If we keep dreaming of the parents that we wish we'd had or the family that every child deserves, we will probably get very upset thinking about the family we grew up in or the way our parents still treat us. Although these daydreams are lovely, and we tell ourselves that thinking this way will make us feel good, the truth is that they are very destructive.

These imaginary worlds, filled with idealized versions of people, where everything is as we would like it to be and where anything is possible, prevent us from living in the real world with our feet on the ground. Reality is not this bright; flesh-and-blood people have flaws and limitations. Although we have options, these are not unlimited. Whenever we compare the world of our dreams with the real world, the real world always comes in a distant second. We will only end up feeling frustrated or disappointed, when we come back down and see that the real world is not at all like our fantasy. Things are just as they are. If we fight against reality, as this is the only one that truly exists, reality will always win.

Humans have an amazing capacity to deny reality. A scene in the surrealist film by director Jose Luis Cuerda, *Dawn Breaks, Which Is No Small Thing* illustrates this idea. An old man lives in a small mountain village in Spain with his grandson, who is a six-foot-tall African young man with black skin. Every day the old man goes downstairs and when he sees the boy, he runs back upstairs screaming in panic, "There's a black man in my house! There's a black man in my house!" The boy answers him, "Grandpa, I am your grandson. I have been living with you for the last 20 years!" The frequency of an event or its obviousness has nothing to do with our willingness to accept its existence. When something does not fit with our previous ideas, when it's not in our idea of how things are, we can refuse to accept that it's like this. But denying reality does not change how it is, just as covering up the moon with your finger does not remove it from the sky. Not accepting things makes it impossible for us to try to change them.

Then what do we have to do with our imaginary planet? Should we destroy it? We don't need to give up our dreams. We simply must embody them and give them shape in the real world. Everything that is represented in our world of ideal things has to do with important, legitimate needs. We all need affection, acceptance, and recognition, to surround ourselves with people that make us feel good and to achieve things in life. All those things are within our reach, but they do not exist in the form of a perfect Prince Charming, but as a flesh-and-blood person we can share and enjoy our life with. They are not in having children who need to achieve everything we were denied, but rather in having children who seek their own goals and develop their potential. They are not found in an illustrious career in a prestigious international firm, but rather in a normal working environment with the typical annoying boss and a nice group of colleagues we get along with and can chat with over a cup of coffee. We don't fight against reality because it's different from our world of dreams, but we learn to identify the elements that were part of our dream world in the world that we have in front of us, and not to reject them because they don't shine as brightly or are not 100% how we would like them to be. Little by little, everything that we were looking for in our dream world will be at hand. And most importantly, it will be real.

The good from evil

Many of the strategies that we have used in order to move forward are not negative in and of themselves. However, at present, they are no longer useful, or they cause us problems. For example, being strong is not a value in itself, but rather a survival mechanism. Forgetting is not a solution; it's only a patch, because we cover up memories, since no such thing as a mental eraser exists. Not reacting is the best we can do when we don't have options, but it can work against us when we do.

Now that we know that many of our supposedly positive beliefs are not so great, let's take a look at the other side of the coin: many of our negative aspects may be better than we think. We may consider some of them to be negative because other people taught us to believe that they were, which can be exacerbated by the moral standards of the society where we live. The concepts of altruism, generosity or the idea that we must be good are imbued with religious overtones. Conversely, selfishness and evil will be labeled as negative. But we already know that nothing is what it seems, so let's reflect on this a little more.

We may think that selfishness is always bad, but this is not true. In some ways, selfishness is to our minds as hunger is to our body. If we are a little selfish, we prioritize what we need over the needs of others. This tendency helps tip the balance in our favor. If we repress all selfish tendencies that we may have, we will always sacrifice our interests for the interests of others. Thus, we usually eat less than we need to, and we become emotionally malnourished. Additionally, if we always tend to be generous, care for others, be altruistic, never say no and yield to the demands of others, it's easy for us to tend to relate to figures that fit with our patterns of functioning - people that ask for more than they give, or who are glad to be cared for by us or who do not care about our needs. For the balance to be well-adjusted, we must be healthily selfish and, at least occasionally, prioritize our needs. We will probably feel bad because of it, but remember: our body and our nervous system will adapt to it, and then sensations will feel better.

Another concept that has a bad reputation is evil. It's unlikely that we define ourselves as evil, but rather as good people. However, we all do bad things from time to time. It's impossible to live without hurting someone. We are not talking about unnecessary or unjustified harm, only to feel powerful by causing harm to others, but the inevitable damage that sometimes we cause by standing up for ourselves and fighting for our rights, to the detriment of others. If we take a competitive exam to secure a place at university or a job in the civil service and we pass, there are others who lose out. If we are completely honest in a job interview, and we don't say what the company expects to hear, we might not get the position. If we allow our opponent to pass us, they'll win. Whenever we compete against others, even if it's a clean fight, someone will end up losing. If we are not a little evil in life, others will, at some point, take advantage of us. Without being a little selfish or fighting for our rights, we won't achieve what matters to us, and we will never prevail in our aims. The people around us are not 100% generous or altruistic either, and if we keep this in mind, we will simply function according to the rules of the game. While reading this, if we feel uncomfortable or disagree, that means we are probably using a point of reference from our imaginary world where justice prevails, and everybody behaves as they should[22].

Other concepts that we may view as negative are that way because our first experience with them was negative or was associated with a bad experience. We have already reflected on how vulnerability is not necessarily negative, but if someone hurts us when we have left our most vulnerable parts in their hands, we can associate danger with vulnerability. For this reason, we don't allow ourselves to show our vulnerability, thus causing ourselves much greater damage. Another similar example is how we understand being weak. If we survived our past by being strong and pushing forward, we can overestimate the positive side of being strong. Additionally, if in our past there was a strong but harmful person who crushed someone who was weak and submissive, we can equate being weak to being damaged. As a result, when we feel weak, we won't rely on anyone and will deprive ourselves of resources which could be useful to us. We will end up trying to do everything without the support of others and tiring easily. When we see ourselves this way, we won't feel good, because being weak is unacceptable, and we may feel angry for not being strong enough.

Other sensations may seem negative simply because they are unpleasant sensations, and we have developed a tendency to avoid them. All the feelings that we avoid will become increasingly intolerable. Our body and our nervous system will have no opportunity to get used to them. For example, if we tend to self-abandon, the sensation of effort may seem unpleasant and stressful. By contrast, if we play a sport, effort is understood as a positive - but not pleasant - sensation, because exerting ourselves is the way to improve our physical condition and performance. If we avoid the sensation of effort, we won't develop our full potential, nor will we get the results that only come with continued effort in the medium and long term. As we have never seen what we can gain from effort, we are unfamiliar with examples that are encouraging when we begin to strive towards something, examples that show us that working hard is worth it. If we are lost in laziness and experiencing the discomfort of personal carelessness, searching for another unpleasant sensation won't seem to make any sense. But by never feeling the sensation of effort or by not seeking it out, we won't learn to handle it and our body won't integrate this fruitful resource.

Another example of a much-needed unpleasant sensation is uncertainty. When it's positively understood, the feeling of uncertainty is very important, since changes, or transitions from one stage to another, are always associated with that sensation. When things are not under our control, we feel a certain insecurity, as we don't know what is about to happen. Remember that in some dysfunctional attachment styles, exploring this territory is not easy. In this case, we lack a sense of inner security, because we did not have a secure base, and as a substitute for true security, we try to control everything. But without exploration there is no learning, and without uncertainty there is no evolution. This is one of the elements of the old adage, "Better the devil you know…" and thus we remain in detrimental situations because we are afraid to trade them in for better - but uncertain - new ones. Taking the risk of changing towards new and better things may seem like looking over the edge of a cliff, unless we learn to get used to uncertainty. If we seek out this sensation - by trying to do things differently, taking alternative routes to get where we're going, having coffee in a different cafe, trying out new recipes, or making small changes in the way we usually do things, even if these changes are unnecessary, we can reconcile ourselves with the feeling of uncertainty and even come to enjoy it. At that point we can improvise, invent, explore, and venture out. As we saw previously, trauma leads to rigidity, and uncertainty is an essential resource that we need to change it.

The elements that need changing are specific for each person. They are those things that make us say "I absolutely can't stand feeling this way." The things that we are least able to tolerate are those which we need to practice the most. If we can't stand things out of place, we have to make ourselves jumble them up a little. If we have to do everything perfectly, we must settle for imperfection and make mistakes on purpose. If we can't cry in front of people, we must learn to share our emotions. Of course, we won't feel good while doing these things, but remember, the important question is this: is this good for us?

18 WORKING ON THE MOST ATROPHIED MUSCLE: REGAINING BALANCE

All situations in which the interrelationships between extremes are involved are the most interesting and instructive. Wilhelm von Humboldt.

Our right hand is no better than our left. We realize the importance of both hands when one of them is injured. It's true that if we are right-handed, this hand dominates in most activities, but we need both of them for many things that we do. This is also true for the majority of mental functions: we need both extremes to achieve a balanced reaction[23]. On some occasions, we are inclined towards one over the other, depending on the situation. If we are prone to one extreme reaction and reject the opposite, this balance will not occur. Some muscles will atrophy while others get overdeveloped, leaving us unbalanced and lopsided. To restore balance, we must train the weaker muscles, and let the others rest, until their strength evens out.

Some situations make us happy, while with others it's logical to feel sad. If we don't have a problem with either of the two emotional states, we will delight in our joy, and let sadness flow easily, while letting ourselves be helped through the comfort of others. The problem may come when we don't allow ourselves to enjoy things, because we tell ourselves that we should only do useful, productive activities, and not waste time. We may be more familiar with sadness, but when it's not balanced out with moments of joy, it becomes deeper and heavier.

Sooner or later, sorrow will grow and overshadow everything else. If this is our case, we have to practice doing things for the simple pleasure of doing them, without worrying about whether or not they are useful for us.

We may believe in some cases that we have to choose between yielding to what others want and giving up on what we want, in order to avoid problems and conflicts with other people. The logical way is to learn to be firm, to say things in a clear but non-offensive way, and to stay calm, but without giving in. Does this seem difficult? If the answer is yes, that means we just need to practice it more. If we are good at caring for others, but asking for what we want is difficult for us, this last psychological muscle is the one we need to build up. We may need to learn, for example, to say no. Let's try saying the word NO out loud and repeating it over and over. If just doing this makes us feel anxious, we must work on this more. By repeating the word "no" 50 times a day, in no time at all, it will feel familiar on our tongue. We can then practice saying "no" in meaningless situations, with people that we are not afraid of, and where consequences don't matter. For example, we can say a clear "no" when the waiter asks us if we want dessert or when the phone company tries to interest us in their latest offer. Later on, we will increase the difficulty of the exercises. Apart from saying no, we must also get used to insisting, and we should do this at least once more than what we would under normal circumstances. It's important not to give up if the other person criticizes our attitude and not to fall back on justifications or make counterattacks. This ability to defend our ideas or say no, without losing control or giving up, is called assertiveness[24]. Of course, once we have developed this muscle, we don't need to do these exercises every day, but we do need use these new skills on a regular basis. Remember that it's normal to fall back on old patterns if new ones are not fully consolidated, and even if they are, we must be vigilant. When this new pattern becomes automated, it will be more natural to give in only when we are convinced about something or when it suits us to do so, and we will say no, or we will ask for what we want, without great difficulties.

Dilemmas that can make us feel trapped are plentiful, and all of them are based on the same false choice: we think about the two options in their most extreme versions, and we debate them with ourselves, bouncing from one extreme to the other. We already know that extremes are never good solutions, but our beliefs can make us think that only one of them is correct, and that moving an inch in the other direction is the same as going all the way to the other side. For example, we can overload ourselves, taking on everything and requiring 110% of ourselves, because we believe that this is our duty or this is what is expected of us. We believe that if we don't do things in a certain way, this will mean that we are irresponsible and a hopeless mess. For example, if we were raised by demanding parents who were constantly disappointed in one of our brothers or sisters because they didn't study or care about anything, and it was up to us to be the responsible child, we may end up overestimating the importance of doing things well; this is what was demanded of us, and this is the role we learned to play. The other extreme, being carefree and irresponsible, will instead have an extremely negative connotation, because our sibling was labeled this way in the family. Being less demanding of ourselves means shouldering less responsibility and being less of a perfectionist. To do this, we must practice being irresponsible and careless, but this reminds us of our brother and makes us feel uncomfortable. We will probably need to remind ourselves that abandoning one extreme does not mean we have to embrace the other. In fact, it's likely that if we continue to function at such an extreme level of fastidiousness and perfectionism, at some stage in our life we will probably be unable to take on further responsibilities or care for anything, because we are stuck in our anxiety or depression, and we no longer have the energy to do so.

If we have lived in extreme environments for a long time, or were raised in them, our responses will also tend to be extreme. We can identify more with one extreme and reject the other, or swing from one end to the opposite. In any case, proportionate responses, which are the ones that work best, are not going to be present. It's important for us to understand the origin of our reactions and plan strategies that help us develop a more balanced response.

For example, if we feel rejection from the people who took care of us, our mind may try to assimilate this in many ways. We can devote all of our energy to seeking their approval, which often does not work very well, because when a parent rejects a child, it's not due to a defect in the child but to significant difficulties in the adult. When we try to please such parents, our efforts will never be enough, and as children we think it's our fault and strive even more to get something we need, but which never comes. As a result, we will become self-demanding perfectionists, and the feeling that "It's never enough" will always be lurking in the background. Another possibility is that we may become hypersensitive to signals of rejection, while we will reject ourselves, and perhaps other people as well. We think that if we say what we feel, if we do what we want, if we allow ourselves to reject others, we will be left alone, and no one will love us. This will shape our personality and make us withdrawn, shy, shameful and compliant. In any case, we must be aware of the roots of our problem. Things worked that way within our family because our parents gave us conditional acceptance. It's important to remind ourselves that our family of origin norms are not the standards that rule the world, and that what happened in our childhood home won't necessarily happen with everyone that we meet afterwards. We may tend to swing from one end to the other, wavering between holding everything in and exploding, between idealizing people and hating them, between sinking into a bad mood and being hyperactive and euphoric, between opening up completely and being defensive, and between engaging and running away. But we will never find the solution we are seeking when we choose one extreme or the other; in fact, trying to do so is where our real problem lies. We are unable to operate in the middle, we bounce between A and Z, as if there were no more letters in the alphabet. The solution is to learn to write with G, L, and N. The important moment is when we notice a tendency, whatever it may be. If we stop it and don't let ourselves get completely carried away, that means we are functioning in a way that is much closer to being in balance.

For example, when we feel elated, we can help ourselves be more realistic by stopping to think about the possible consequences of our ideas. When we feel discouraged, we should try to do the opposite and remind ourselves of the positive things in our lives. We don't open up in front of someone we barely know, nor do we strike a person from our list of friends when they do something that we don't like; we protect ourselves and at the same time, remain in relationships. This ability to be open while at the same time maintain some distance can be difficult when we tend to have extreme and opposite reactions, because at one end, we see all the good things in the other person, while at the other end, we can only see the negatives. Something that can help us when we are in one emotional state is to write ourselves a letter about what is important to remember in the other state. For example, if we feel disappointed with someone because after giving our all in the relationship, we did not get back what we expected, we will explain to ourselves in the letter why we have to take better care of ourselves in the next relationship, and not care so much about the other person. If we tend to do irresponsible or risky things as an extreme reaction, and we feel guilty about it, we can write down the reasons why we shouldn't do it again and push ourselves to read this letter the next time we want to do the same.

Another possibility would be to observe where we oscillate between one extreme and the other, and sit down and figure out an intermediate reaction which has a little bit of both. Some examples would be how to take a stance without giving in or losing control, or what we could talk about if we opened ourselves up to another person without completely divulging our deepest secrets. We could think about what we would stop doing when taking care of others, for example, if instead of giving them 100% of ourselves, we gave them 80%. We must be specific in describing these alternatives, imagine them in detail, see ourselves doing them, and then practice them. As with every healthy change, we will probably feel very uncomfortable at the beginning, because the underlying tendency continues to operate, but over time, the feelings will become more positive.

In any case, it's important when trying to change any functioning pattern to first observe without making negative judgments, and understand how we got to the place where we are, and second, to begin to work on the thing we normally try to avoid or reject. Again, as we mentioned with Destin and his bike, we have to try a thousand times, and assume that we will fail repeatedly, but nevertheless, we must persist until a new pattern starts to form and solidifies.

The process we have been following to come to terms with ourselves, which means accepting the different aspects of our personality and helping them to evolve from the initial models to our personal new style, helps us find a new balance. Usually when we notice very different aspects about ourselves, when we have a strong internal battle, each part of the conflict represents an extreme position. These parts of our personality can stop fighting over which part is better and join forces towards common goals.

Any reaction that is too intense must be reduced, but in general, it will be difficult to do so if we are in a state of great emotional intensity. The trick is to make the changes before these reactions occur. For example, fits of rage can be prevented by becoming angry more often and more productively. If we allow ourselves to notice these everyday small annoyances and do something about them - meaning that we talk about them calmly, step away from the situation that bothers us or choose to react in another way - rage won't build up inside us. By doing so, our anger will be less likely to explode out of control. If not, we will feel like a pressure cooker with a blocked valve, and we all know what will end up happening… We have to open the valve. This way, things will cook properly.

Consider the following example: Our mother is an anxious woman who is always worried about everything, and we dutifully call her every day. We don't want to call her so often, it doesn't seem reasonable now that we are in our forties, but if we don't, we will have to deal with her criticism. Whenever we call, we are rebuked just the same, so we like calling her even less, although we continue to do so. When we talk with her, we bite our tongue and refrain from saying what we really think. One day, perhaps because of something insignificant, we finally blow up, yell at her, and then - while crying - she tells us that we have the same intolerable personality as our father. As we have suffered because of our authoritarian father, we feel bad about both our reaction and our mother's comment, so we tell ourselves that we need to avoid conflicts and disagreements, because we can't manage them. We feel terrible and say that we'll never let ourselves get like that again.

What would the solution be? Of course, torturing ourselves for months because of our behavior won't solve much. If we do something productive with our anger from the beginning, we can introduce a change. Everything starts when we notice that our mother's dependence bothers us, and we stand firm by not calling her as often, despite her saying "You're a bad son, you think only of yourself." We remind ourselves that she's right, that being a little bad is healthy, and that it's also important to think about our wants and needs. If we don't do that, we will start feeling agitated or distressed, and not only will we feel bad, but we will also end up reacting poorly towards others. We can trust that our mind will adjust to these feelings if we allow ourselves to feel this guilt and discomfort without getting sucked into a vicious cycle. We can't escape our feelings, but we also shouldn't let them run our lives either. We let our rage help us, we allow ourselves to feel it, and we follow the tendency underlying that emotion. After some time - remember, eight months if we practice daily - even if others do not modify the way they function, we will feel very different. And sometimes, interestingly, unexpected changes in others may occur. But this is something extra - it's important to remember that this is not our main objective.

An important point regarding learning to move towards the middle zones is to understand that, for some time, everything we do will be a bit sloppy. If we are compliant and tend to submit to others, getting good and angry, with conviction, self-control, class and elegance, is not going to happen immediately. In the beginning we might lose control a bit, or maybe we'll do it timidly or anxiously or not know how much to tighten the reins to keep our reaction under control. Since we are rehearsing a type of conduct that we have been holding back for a long time, in the first attempts we may go a bit overboard. It's important for us to refine our responses but also to be aware that these are only our first attempts at this and that we must practice a lot in order to master them. Therefore, it's good to try this out with minor issues and in inconsequential situations, rather than going directly - this would be our typical extremism - to more complex situations. In general, it tends to be easier to establish these changes in new relationships, than with those that are already associated with certain behavioral habits. The hardest thing will be to change the style with the people most associated with the learning of our old patterns, such as our family of origin or people we have problematic relationships with. If we start with the simplest things, when we get to something complex, we will already have incorporated many new resources, and tested them long enough to have them quite integrated into our behavioral repertoire.

Another aspect to consider is that if we have suppressed a way of being, acting, thinking or feeling for a long period of time, when we finally allow ourselves to experience it, we may think that this is the final goal and the we are already okay. In fact, we have gone from one end of the spectrum to the other, without being aware of this. Especially when the initial situation was an unpleasant feeling, we can confuse the new feeling of positive tone with a healthy state. Here are some examples.

Fighting for everything and not tolerating anything might make us believe that we are defending our rights and proving that we are self-confident. This occurs if we have always been timid and have avoided all conflict and confrontation. However, it doesn't make sense to fight every battle, and this attitude will end up putting distance between us and others. Sometimes we may decide not to fight, not because we are not justified in doing so, but because it's not worthwhile or not in our interest, and these issues are also important to consider.

If we usually hold back our rage, and now we start to allow ourselves to feel it, we can confuse being abrupt, hostile and even rude with being assertive and firm. When we talk about things we don't agree with or when we have to confront someone, it's important to respect the other person, even if they don't do the same; otherwise we will get down to their level. It's also necessary to listen to the others' arguments, because even though we are convinced of our position, we can also make mistakes. Defending our ideas and maintaining an open dialogue are not mutually exclusive.

When we feel insignificant, inferior, or worthless, and we start reasserting ourselves, we can begin to enjoy feelings that we previously denied ourselves, such as standing out, winning, being dominant, feeling power and strength, and feeling a sense of control over others. These emotional states can be addictive, and even more so if we have never allowed ourselves to experience them. The internal feeling may be one of euphoria, of an intense sensation of well-being, or of all problems seeming to disappear. We may no longer want to feel like we did before, and we now believe that we have the right to experience these new exciting sensations after all the suffering that the world has put us through. This is actually not the best version of ourselves - it's just the other extreme of our previous problem. If we continue like this, we will see that it has many secondary effects. Others will get denesive around us, and it will be harder for us to establish relationships and really connect. We will disconnect from our vulnerability, with all the negative effects that we have already mentioned that disconnecting brings about.

The same thing can occur with all extreme tendencies when we start to modify them. If we were extremely shy, we can go overboard in the other direction. If we didn't use to express our emotions of sadness or pain, we may become overwhelmed when we let them out. If we used to feel overly convinced of ourselves or overly confident, we may start doubting everything. If we used to be easily triggered and reacted impulsively and aggressively, we may see ourselves as too fragile and exposed when we show our vulnerable parts. If we stop functioning in a very self-reliant manner, we may feel extremely dependent on people that we have ventured to form a bond with. These feelings can be strange because we have left known territory, lacking references, and that means that we are doing well. We are daring ourselves to explore.

It's important to know that these sensations won't always be like this. In a second stage, we will learn to familiarize ourselves with the new feelings, and to calibrate and mold our responses. If we understand this as a period of transition, we will see ourselves with greater understanding, but also with some degree of self-criticism. It's very likely that those around us, who are accustomed to us being complacent and never opposing anything, will make a fuss and question our changes, not because they are bad, but because it goes against the status quo they were comfortable with. But somehow, feedback from others can also give us crucial information about how to learn to do things in a more nuanaced, flexible way, how to set boundaries, and how to reaffirm or express our emotions and opinions.

In some cases, the response from our environment may push us back to old patterns, expressing rejection toward our new attitudes, using phrases such as, "You've been acting terrible lately," "You're crazy," or "Lately no one has been able to put up with you." It's important to question their statements, especially when some of those people are the ones who contributed to the development of our internal patterns. For example, if we were raised by a bitter, dissatisfied mother, anything we do will never be good enough for her, so when she puts up a fuss, it won't mean anything, as she has been putting up a fuss her entire life. Or if we had an overly-dominant father, he will penalize us for rebelling, because only our submission would be acceptable for him. These people's comments are the ones which affect us the most, because they are intrinsically linked to our past and our problems, but this does not mean that their opinions are truer than those of others. The most valuable and neutral opinions are probably those coming from people outside our family. It's also important to take into account those people who don't say anything in particular or who find our evolution positive.

If we evolve, the environment has to adjust to our changes, and this adaptation is sometimes fluent and natural, but at other times we will find more inflexibility and will need to oil the pieces that squeak when they get moved from their usual position. Any movement in a system can initially generate a response within that system that is an attempt to return to homeostasis, to its previous state of equilibrium. But if we were the ones who suffered the consequences for that state of equilibrium, if we lost out or endured hardship, we are the ones who have to lead the transition. If the system is flexible, after some time it will adapt. If it's very rigid, we need to maintain our position for a long time or completely upend the system. Let's remember that as adults, we can also move to another system, put other elements in it, or consider different options. The only thing that does not makes sense is to keep maintaining things the way they are, when they make us unhappy.

19 THE TURNING POINT

No decision is, in itself, a decision. William James.

Perhaps we are reading this book and thinking, "Yes, I'd have to change many things." But that's not the only thing that is necessary to feed good - it's necessary to decide to do it. We must be determined to change things, to do what is needed to change our perspectives, and to bet on ourselves. Doing this is not easy with the kinds of problems that we are talking about.

Many people who have lived through negative situations in their families of origin, with their partners, or in other significant relationships remain trapped and lament their fate but don't make a move. What has happened to them seems unforgivable, and they think that as a result, they have to be permanently angry. They feel the world has treated them unfairly, wonder why they were the ones who had to have those negative experiences, and think they are victims of bad luck or that fate is against them. They sometimes go to therapy, but not because they are looking for change, but rather so that someone will listen to them and understand all their past and present suffering.

We can also rebel against the idea that, even if it was others who harmed us, we are the ones who have to change. We may say in therapy, "They are the ones who should be here, they only think about themselves." We may feel that if everything in the world functioned properly, these things would never happen. We may think that this is the way we are, and so we cannot or do not want to change. We are too certain of our opinions on this, and in many respects, we are probably right. But worrying too much about being right is one of the traps we can get caught in, and this keeps us from moving forward. Because, no matter how right we are, what's the point of fretting over how unfair the world is or asking ourselves how people are capable of doing certain things? Does telling ourselves over and over again what other people should change really solve anything? We don't take steps in any direction. We are stuck. Our feeling of powerlessness grows.

This feeling of powerlessness is equivalent to revving our car's engine with the handbrake on. The more we step on the gas, the more the engine revs, but the car doesn't move. Our urge pushes us to change the situation, to do something, but since we only consider impractical solutions, it's like heading towards a dead end. We're left pumping the brakes or trying to drive in a straight line, hoping that the curves in the road disappear or that construction workers will fill in the potholes before we hit one. We complain about our bad luck, but we don't search for an alternative route or a different system, because we tell ourselves that we aren't the ones who should fix the problem. If we talk to ourselves intensely and with conviction, our thoughts may seem like undeniable truths. We don't broaden our perspective; in fact, we resist when others try and say that they don't understand us or they don't understand what we've been through. We cling to our beliefs, and this keeps us stuck in a situation we don't like.

Sometimes these feelings are due to an emotional blockage that is less conscious. Maybe the first times when we felt this way were situations where there were no options, situations where we couldn't face the people who caused them. We had to contain our fight-or-flight response, which is our instinctive way of taking action to protect ourselves. This instinct remained within us, feigning a response that was never allowed to develop. That blockage has remained associated with that protection response until now, even when we are faced with situations where we do have options. We can't see what options are there, and if we do see them, something within us that we don't understand keeps us from acting.

For example, if we suffered abuse as a child, we may have felt an inner cry of, "Stop, stop!" that never escaped our mouths. Maybe we dreamed of running away, but as a child, the option to leave home and start our own life was just not available. As we said at the beginning of this book, a lion cub never challenges the head of the pride; the wisdom of its species is inside him and inhibits the instinct to fight that he carries in his genes. It's not the time for that. The lion cub also knows he can't leave the group, as he can't survive on its own. No doubt that when the cub grows up, he will be able to go up against the lion who dominated him, and if he does, he will most likely be able to defeat the older lion. It's just a matter of letting nature guide you and waiting for the right moment. Humans tend to overcomplicate things. Our most valuable resource, which is our capacity to reflect, makes us think about what could happen and sometimes creates a mental knot that is hard to undo. We feel bad for not having reacted, for not having defended ourselves, for not having left. The lion cub doesn't think about such things, which is why his systems do not get blocked. When he grows up, he won't hate the memory of what he was like when he was little, and he won't feel a sense of rejection towards his inner lion self for being fragile and vulnerable. He will still be able to play when he is relaxed, he will allow himself to be with others of his kind, and when he is with them, he will be able to be calm and simply enjoy the contact. He won't say to himself, "If I don't allow myself to be vulnerable, they can't hurt me again." He will simply let his claws and teeth grow and will feel, deep in every molecule of his body, that he can protect himself if necessary, and that he is getting bigger and stronger. He will practice his alpha roar.

Humans sometimes try to change the natural order of things. We keep our rage contained and analyze its moral aspects. We feel bad about letting ourselves feel anger, because it reminds us of the aggressive people that we used to know and our first models of what anger looked like. Our mind internalizes the significant figures in our history, and from this basis it establishes an internal standard of emotional regulation. As we said, initially we self-care in the same way that we were cared for, and we govern ourselves as others governed us. If our rage turns against us, if we always push it down, only letting it out when it overflows and explodes, we won't be able to develop like the lion cub does, by being in contact with our strength; the cub practices defending himself and fighting through play fighting, and by emulating this, we can learn how to fight when it is the right time to do so. Alternatively, if we identify with aggressive figures and attack everything that surrounds us, we are trying to be adult lions before our bodies are strong enough to support us in the fight. Interestingly, when we do this, we aren't protecting ourselves more, because we attack those we can easily control or those who try to help us, but not those who hurt us the most or, when we can face them, the consequences are more damaging than what we want to protect ourselves from.

The blockage of these reactions probably does not occur only because of what we think about them. Like emotions, the regulation of our reactions largely occurs outside of our consciousness. Active responses to harmful situations may be instinctively blocked, because before we can become consciously aware of it, internally we feel that they are not appropriate for the context. These action tendencies never come to fruition and thus remain undeveloped attempts, but they don't go away either. In some way, it's as if the anger that the fight response is built on turns into tension and powerlessness. The fear that mobilizes the flight response gets stuck in the body, constantly feeding feelings of concern and anxiety. When facing new situations that trigger our survival instinct, these reactions get activated with their associated blockage. When we have to react, we feel helpless and run away, despite the fact that we have the necessary resources in our possession to deal with the situation. As much as we blame ourselves for our weakness and cowardliness, we can't undo these knots; on the contrary, when we get angry at ourselves, we only make the knots tighter.

This does not mean that nothing can be done, but if we want to do something, the first step is to understand what is happening. As we said before, we can only make a change take place when we understand and accept ourselves. Precisely because many of these reactions are automatic processes of which we aren't fully aware, allowing them to flow spontaneously won't help resolve the situation. If we feel trapped in patterns that we dislike or that aren't good for us, we must be determined to make changes and actively work towards achieving them. As we know where the problem is, we must push in the right direction and go through the door that is open and leads to where we really need to go. It's not unusual for us to waste energy by seeking solutions which are impossible, getting angry with ourselves for being wrong or refusing to change situations that hurt us. In order to make the most of our efforts, we should focus on the key elements of the problem, and we have to be willing to change our beliefs, our way of relating to others, and even our definition of who we are. All these elements involve an active decision and a commitment to ourselves to make a profound change in those patterns. It's common for many years of intense discomfort to go by until we reach this turning point and say: "I can't keep doing things this way." The decision itself does not bring about the change we are seeking, but without this decision, change is impossible.

The decision gets made one day and must be adhered to by maintaining a constant commitment to our goal. We can say to ourselves, "This far and no further, I have to change," and turn this into a firm determination, which we work to maintain against all odds, even if at times we might waver. Or we say, "I have to take hold of the reins of my life," and grip them tightly afterwards, no matter how difficult the road ahead may be. But it makes no sense to say things like that if they don't go hand in hand with practical changes. So that this decision will become a true commitment to ourselves and to the change we seek to make, we have to safeguard ourselves against the endless doubts, obstacles and negative tendencies that will emerge along the way. It's important for this to be a thoughtful decision that takes into account the difficulties we have, any unsuccessful attempts that we have already made, and the circumstances that work against us. It's not only a question of unfurling the sails of our ship, but of being able to navigate in any kind of wind or weather.

Making a decision involves many things, and regardless of how clear our decision to change is, we may notice a sense of inertia that pulls us back to our old ways, so we must always stay in "manual mode" and not allow ourselves to fall back on our automatic ways. If we let go of the reins, the old patterns will re-emerge. This is especially true when something unsettles us or when our mood darkens. When this happens, and we are just beginning to learn how to sail, in the middle of the storm, our rudder can wobble. This is just like Destin and his bike; when he got momentarily distracted, he lost his newly acquired skill. These ups and downs, which sometimes can mean one step forward and two steps back, are part of the normal process of learning or rather, of re-learning.

A long list of excuses and dysfunctional beliefs can seep into our mind and take control. Statements like, "I can't" or "I feel really bad now," can reappear. We are actually saying to ourselves that no matter how much we have learned or changed, this time there is nothing we can do. Our experience contradicts the belief, and we have many recent examples to back that up, but it's as if our mind has erased every memory of our achievements, resources and new abilities. This is the moment we read the letter that we wrote to ourselves at that time when we were feeling better; this letter remind us of our goals, of how far we have come, and how we can move past feelings like the ones we have at present. We need to have plans to handle these moments when we feel discouraged, because they will come for sure. Solid improvement depends more on how we handle the bad days than the good ones.

Another aspect which is extremely important in our improvement process is not to leave any issue unresolved. Sometimes when we get better, we declare ourselves "cured" without having worked on the roots of the problem or without having dismantled all the life scripts that are in the basis of our difficulties. We just enjoy our state of well-being, and we don't want to think about our difficulties or problems. Once again, we go back to our usual way of pushing ahead and acting as if nothing is wrong. We don't work on our painful memories because we are afraid to do so, but doing this is the same as building a new house with flimsy materials on a weak foundation. We might feel fine inside the house, and on the outside, it might look much better than the old one, but just like the tale of the three little pigs, a house made of straw will be blown down when life brings new complications. We will not improve if we tell ourselves that everything will work out just fine and that we don't have any problems. Denying the fact that difficulties could arise is as problematic as thinking that everything will go wrong in the future and that the same adverse situations from the past will happen over and over again. Many different things may happen to us throughout our life, and this won't be a problem if our resources to deal with them are well established. A stable change requires us to choose solid materials for our house and to make sure it has a strong foundation, so it will be a place where we feel safe when the weather is bad. But it also must let the sunlight in when the storm ends and the sun comes out.

But it is not only the inertia of the past which can hinder our evolution. Many things may come in the future that push us back or put obstacles in our way. A part of us can believe that we don't deserve to feel good, because we still feel guilty or ashamed about our past experiences or the way that we react to them. We may feel afraid, because improving involves going into the areas of our life that we have pushed off to one side or never dealt with, such as engaging in relationships, coping with conflicts, fighting for what we want or leaving many things behind. Starting to feel better also involves taking responsibility for our life, which is indeed fantastic, but at the same time, it may feel like a burden which we aren't quite ready to handle.

The decision to work towards bettering ourselves and everything that this process entails, including the length of time it may take, must be made whole-heartedly. Every part of us must agree on this decision. It's essential to reach a consensus and make a pact with ourselves. It's better to take smaller steps and move forward by carrying our inner child, our critical part and everything else that we are, with us. To do this, we need to talk to ourselves and understand our contradictions and deeply held beliefs. Some thoughts are difficult to modify, even after working on the many memories that fed them. When we live through adverse, difficult situations for a long period of time, these sensations put down deep roots, and pulling them out takes time. We must have infinite patience with ourselves, understand how difficult it is for our body to relearn something new, and completely let go of all the old patterns. Let's remember that it took Destin only two hours to feel comfortable riding his regular bike, because the old circuits were still there. So, if we see ourselves taking a step backwards one day, we need to remember our firm decision to move forward and head down the path as planned.

A realistic decision also involves relying on people and resources that can help us on our journey; we need supplies, food and water for travelling, and we need to know which ports we can stop at to refuel. Throughout our life, if we have tried to function without getting help from anyone, we need to learn that many things are easier when we can count on the support of others. Choosing the most difficult route increases the likelihood that we will fail. Of course, we need to choose wisely when we ask someone for help, and to what extent to resort to it. But what no one else can ever do for us is make the decision described in this chapter, or commit to the change that we ourselves need to make. If we are not determined to change things, no matter how much help we have or how good it is, it won't do us any good.

20 LOOKING AT THE PAST FROM THE PRESENT

We, of that time, are no longer the same. Pablo Neruda.

Let’s go back and take another look at our memories. We’ve been working on all the changes we’ve talked about, and now we understand more about what is happening to us, and we are getting along with our emotional states and our internal parts better. We’ve also thought a bit about our history and our experiences, some of which still cause us intense pain. It becomes hard to relive those situations, and by doing so, the blockage that separated them from our conscience and from our daily life is once again activated. This can discourage us and result in us pushing them to one side, but we already know that this doesn’t work, so what can we do?

It's important to keep in mind that the fear or sense of rejection that memories and their associated sensations produce in us are deceiving. In all likelihood, when those situations were unfolding, we felt that we could not endure them, that they were unacceptable. When we recall that time, the same thoughts come with the memories, but now - if our internal system is indeed working differently - we are more prepared to deal with them. We can at least stop trying to escape our past experiences and start working on our history. When we turn to face the dark ghosts of our past head on, they end up being less terrifying than we imagined. It’s important to remember that our body and our nervous system can get used to feelings if we allow them to remain there long enough. In fact, one of the therapeutic strategies that can help us is progressive exposure to memories that we have been avoiding for a long time.

Sometimes, when our disconnection is more intense or profound, we aren't aware that a memory still affects us or to what extent it does. We know that it happened, but we don't comprehend its meaning or realize how great an impact it has on what is happening to us now. Not all memories are equally accessible; some can be so blocked off that we don't even know that they are there. In this case, the process requires a preliminary step, which is an attempt to connect to these networks of memories that are partially or totally dissociated from our consciousness.

Sometimes stopping to carefully evaluate memories can help to strengthen the connection. If we think for a minute about a situation that we believe we have overcome, and observe our bodily sensations, we may notice residual feelings that have previously gone unnoticed. We must take a full sixty seconds to stop and examine our body from head to toe, and notice our breathing, our posture, any areas of tension or heaviness, any sensations in our chest or belly, or anything else that we feel inside. We often overlook our feelings without realizing they are there. We can place our open hand over the area where we notice the greatest feeling of discomfort.

If there is even the smallest difference between what we notice then, and what we feel when we think about something totally neutral, that means those feelings are important, and we must pay attention to them. If we don't notice anything, we can place our hand on our chest or our belly, and just observe our breathing. While doing this, we can think about caring for our feelings, without trying to remove them, pushing them or pressuring ourselves. The aim of this exercise is simply to learn to look inwards, to stop and examine our inner feelings, and to observe them while thinking about taking care of them, and not avoiding or suppressing them. In doing so, we may not notice anything, or we might notice sensations and see how they are regulated, or observe how our thoughts interfere and cause our emotions to rise, fall or change. It's important to be clear that this is not an exercise in relaxation, but a moment of self-observation and connection. It will produce an effect only if we do it regularly, and through progressive and patient learning.

Another important element regarding memories that are not

completely processed is being able to share these experiences, which in many cases we may have shared with no one, or at least not with anyone who could understand how we feel. In some cases, our tendency to keep pushing ahead made us not want to talk about everything that happened, so that the memories would not come back. Other times, our distrust of other people did not make it easy for us to tell them. It's possible that some of these memories can cause feelings of deep shame or self-loathing and therefore, this makes it difficult for us to reveal them. Or perhaps we have never had anyone to share our sorrow and grief with, and it's hard for us to do it now. But sharing the pain is the best way to ease it, by allowing ourselves to feel understanding and comfort from others. To do this, we must learn to speak about our pain, but not from the rage we protect ourselves with, or the multiple walls that we have built to protect ourselves from this pain.

Some therapies can help us in a specific way, even when our memories are blocked or when the feelings do not fade away after we face these memories. One such example is EMDR therapy[25], which has been scientifically shown to be effective in processing traumatic memories. By using eye movements or other forms of alternating tactile or auditory stimulation of the brain, our processing system can be unlocked, and then integrate the experience that has been isolated. This mechanism seems to be similar to the one that is present during one of the phases of sleep called REM (rapid eye movement), which has been associated with storing emotional memories. This therapy generates changes not only in our way of looking at the situation, but also in our emotions and physical sensations.

Working with memories usually requires a kind of therapy that is specially designed to treat traumatic experiences[26]. A generic psychotherapeutic treatment can be useful in many ways, but it is necessary to deal with the specific situations that have contributed to creating the problem. It's difficult to do this without help; in fact, it would be like trying to operate on ourselves. In a certain way, processing a traumatic memory is similar to cleaning a wound that has long been infected. Once it is done, we may feel a great sense of relief, because it will stop hurting and can heal, and as a result, it will no longer consume our energy. But the process is complex, sometimes painful and difficult, and often requires a professional with a clinical background to intervene. Accepting help, when help can make things easier, is just as important as taking charge of our recovery process.

The same problems that arise when we seek support in another person, when we try to confide in someone or when we interact with people, and that were described when we talked about sharing our experiences with others, can be activated when working with a therapist. The difference is that the therapist is prepared to understand our difficulties and to help us to overcome them. The support provided by a friend or someone else who is close to us is different than the support of a professional, but these two types of support do complement one another. In both cases, they will transmit something to us that we probably did not have when the worst things in our life were happening: the feeling that there is another human being that understands what is happening to us, and who can relate to it. Adverse situations where we have the support of others tend not to get blocked up so easily, and we assimilate them better. It's as if human contact counteracts the negative impact of experiences. Even if we did not have this at that time, sharing it now can be an emotional experience that modifies the memory of that situation in a powerful way. That is why it is worthwhile to overcome our fears and reticence, and work to get beyond our difficulties. When the history that we carry inside us is very complex, it's especially important for us not to try to do all this work by ourselves.

At the same time, it's essential for us to help prepare the way. It's wrong to rule out the idea of professional help because "We don't believe in therapy," often without ever having tried it or only having gone to a couple of sessions with a therapist. But it's also wrong to expect them to "get rid of" feelings of discomfort and unease. A therapist does not have magical powers, nor can they make our problems disappear, if we don't take an active role in our own changing process. If we understand that facing our experiences is fundamental, when the right time to do it presents itself, we can begin to explore some of the resources we have available to us.

Something that seems obvious, but that may not be, is that when we connect with our memories, we must experience them as such. This means that while we are noticing all the feelings that they still produce, our mind does not get confused thinking that the event is happening again. Some memories are so vivid or have been locked up and isolated for so long, that when they come back, it seems to us - literally - like we are reliving the situation. We have to repeatedly remind our mind that it is only a memory and that it is not happening again, that however unpleasant reconnecting with those feelings can be, it has been a long time since then. We must also be aware of the difference between that time and this time, because it is important for us to know that those circumstances are over, that it's not going to happen anymore or that it won't happen again in the same way. For example, something that happened in childhood can't happen again in the same way in adulthood, not because the situation cannot reoccur, but because we are no longer at that life stage. The danger in childhood, when we are totally dependent on the people who take care of us, is over. Of course, to be able to say this, we have to work with the feeling of defenselessness and of being very little, a feeling that still gets the better of us. We need to learn how to take care of that sensation, try new ways to protect ourselves, and work on modifying our internal structure. So, when we say to ourselves, "It's just a memory, things are different now, I am an adult, I'm learning to protect myself," we can believe our statements.

It's also important not to take the thoughts that come with the memories as literal truths. We may think, "I want to die" not so much because we consider this possibility now, but because it was what we felt when that situation happened in the past. Perhaps we have the feeling that nobody will support us, because this is what we thought at that time, and it was the main reason why our mind blocked that experience. We may believe that we are in danger, even though we now know that there is no danger, because we feel fear, and our brain makes us believe that feeling afraid is equal to being in danger. These beliefs that come with the memories can be intense, as intense as the emotional and somatic part of the memories, but they are only thoughts that were stored with the experience in our brain. It's important that we see them as such, and not take them as if they were absolute truths.

The past and the present memory networks can "talk" with each other, help one another and become integrated if we can look at the memory with the full awareness of being here and connect with the sensations, emotions, and beliefs of that time. At the same time we should keep in mind that we are in a new stage of life, that we have learned many things, that the situation is different and, above all, that we are different. The adult we are now will meet the child we once were, the person working to get better will be able to take care of the part of them that remains blocked, and we will look at the past from the perspective of the present. Our way of looking at this must come from a place of patience and empathy, without any form of judgment, and we must be open to understanding everything that happened. We don't go back to our past experiences to look at ourselves in the same way that we were looked at, but with our fresh, wiser eyes. We rescue our self from the past where it was stuck, and we bring it to the present moment, in which new possibilities begin to open up.

The way in which the past can stop influencing the present is just the opposite of what we sometimes think. If the past was difficult and complex, trying to leave it behind, moving forward so our memories cannot reach us or burying them deep inside ourselves is not useful in the long run. The only way to really overcome those experiences is to embrace who we are now, make peace with who we were at the various stages of our life, and understand what we did and what we weren't able to do. When we integrate our distressing memories, the pain will begin to leave us; it will become diluted in the rest of our experiences, no longer be isolated and will be connected with new life experiences.

Our worst memories can stop hurting us and become truly neutral memories which do not affect us. We can achieve this change without striving to disconnect, trying to push them aside or devoting our mental energy to keeping them under control. It's possible to leave the past behind without the risk of reactivating it in the context of present-day situations. We can deactivate the landmines in our garden and make it a place that is safe and can be enjoyed. Some people are reluctant to get to the bottom of their most difficult experiences, because they do not believe that it is possible to remove the pain brought on by them. They are too frightened, or they believe that they will be damaged forever, and that their painful sensations will never end. It's important to know that this is not so, and that there are many alternatives that can help change those residual feelings associated with memories.

If we have difficult experiences in our past and do not work on them, we not only allow them to influence both our current life and our future, but somehow, we also leave the child or the person we were when that happened trapped in the sensations of that time. We abandon a part of ourselves and condemn it to continue living in these situations. In order for the person we are now to disconnect from that pain and move forward, a part of our mind had to stay there. If we don't examine it, if we don't embrace and get that part of ourselves back, we end up leaving it to its own fate, doing nothing or blaming that part of ourselves for what happened. By doing this, we reenact what other people did to us and the way they dealt with the problem we had. We repeat, internally, the same thing we suffered because of others. Furthermore, if we don't get back in touch with that part, we will never feel complete, and the main risk of this is that even if we do feel better, this improvement will not be solid and stable. It's like knowingly leaving that active landmine buried in the backyard.

Certainly we have to find the right moment and sometimes, after working hard to change and improve things, if we start to feel better we may - as we said before - feel reluctant to get into the hard part of our personal biography, and turn things upside down when we have worked so hard to get to get to this point. This is understandable, and we need to feel strong and stable in order to take this on. It's also beneficial to have a period of peace to cement these changes.

Above all, it's essential to pace the process and understand that it has different stages. Work on the most traumatic memories must be done on a secure base, propped up on a strong emotional cushion. Just as if we were going to be operated on, infections must be cured beforehand, and our body has to be well-nourished, strong and stable. Wanting to go too quickly is just as detrimental as letting ourselves be guided only by our fear. Deciding when is a good time to address our traumas is not simple at all, and the best guideline is break it up and space it out over time. It often helps reduce the difficulty of our therapeutic process by leaving time for emotions to settle, continuing with the changes in our daily life, and progressively approaching the most complex or difficult aspects. In addition, it's a good way to respect our limitations and consider our needs, without abandoning or ignoring what is happening to us.

Working little by little on our memories usually helps us make changes, in addition to the daily life changes that we are making. For example, if we have difficulties managing our anger and we manage to describe the situations of violence that we experienced, changing the way we feel when we remember them and the perspective from which we do it, surely our anger management will change without the need to do it through a conscious exercise. Each process improves the other. If we don't work on taking better care of ourselves, regulating our emotions and relating to others in a different way, then working with our past is probably not enough to change all these things. But if we try to improve our self-care patterns without reflecting on the experiences of being cared for in previous significant relationships, we are probably going to notice much more inertia toward the old patterns and blockage when we try to change them. Joining efforts in both directions, and working on memories and present patterns at the same time, is the most effective strategy.

After all the work that involves modifying problematic patterns, inherited beliefs and feelings attached to old experiences, it would be a shame if we didn't do a general cleaning, empty closets and drawers, and get rid of everything that is not ours. It's important for us to reclaim any aspects of ourselves that we have forgotten, hidden, denied or rejected; but it's also very relevant to disown outdated models, slogans and family rules that we don't agree with, customs that we don't like, and memories that are still interfering. A memory that has not passed to the file of neutral issues and still has active emotions, feelings and beliefs attached to it is one that consumes our energy, even when we are not recalling it on a regular basis. Once unlocked and transferred to the general storage, it will look like an old picture in a photo album. When this album is complete, we will be able to write a complete history of our life and include all its chapters. Doing this will also allow us to see it as a whole, from a distance and with perspective. This new narrative about our history will shed light on many aspects that we have only partially understood, like analyzing the pieces of a puzzle, putting some together, and just intuiting what picture they form. After processing different experiences, that image will become clearer. By approaching these memories this way, we don't get absorbed or trapped by them, but they will become part of our experience, our learning, and the history that has brought us to the present and made us who we are. Looking at them from this new perspective lets us be freer to evolve in different directions. However, if we leave drawers unopened, we make it easier for what's inside them to upend us later, getting caught off guard by disturbing sensations when unexpected memories surface in our mind.

Finally, although we have done a thorough job on our experiences, these unexpected recollections may still happen, sometimes because there were areas of our history that we did not review or because some circumstances may trigger underlying memories. In any case, we will always have time to complete the work. Recovering from long and difficult experiences is not the same as finishing a ten-day course of antibiotics. It's a process that will always be part of our lives, since we are constantly evolving, and so are the situations we find ourselves in.

21 OUR INTERNAL PARTS VERSION 2.0

The curious paradox is that when I accept myself just as I am, then I can change. Carl Rogers.

As we start understanding ourselves, relearning to feel, taking care of ourselves, and taking the situation by the reins, our feelings also change and evolve. The various aspects of our internal world begin to fit together better and become more appropriate for the time we are living in, and we can identify better with who we really are. The parts that make up our personality develop to their full potential and let us see resources that we have, but were previously unaware of. Although this is not yet happening, it's good for us to imagine what the route will be like, and how each of these parts can regenerate and become an improved version of themselves. Here we will describe some possibilities that should merely serve as a guide. Each one of us needs to figure out the distinct aspects we are made of, how and why they developed, and the possibilities they contain. The road is going to be quite similar: understanding the origins of these aspects, removing them from the mold in which they were formed, opening communication with the rest of the system, combining past and present perspectives, and letting them acquire a new form, which better fits with the other parts and the present moment.

Deconstructing the Hulk

In the version of the classic superhero film by director Ang Lee, we can see the story of an enraged Green Monster, who arises from the protagonist's traumatic past and resides within him, explodes without control, and finally evolves into a hero who is able to channel all his anger towards significant ends. During his childhood, the protagonist saw how his father, who used him as a guinea pig for his experiments, killed his mother while they were having a fight. This terrible memory gets locked away in his mind and remains encapsulated along with all the accumulated rage that the child was never able to express. When he was young, he would look at himself in the mirror and see something inside - a green reflection, a hidden part - which was kept out of his consciousness during the day. At night the anguish of the memories would assail him in the form of nightmares which were always the same but never made any sense.

The protagonist, locked away in his rage, is unable to connect emotionally with others, even with his loved ones. He does not defend himself, and emotionally lives only half of the life that he could live. One day something happens that touches him deep inside, and that hidden and buried part escapes out of control. But, fortunately, someone sees him, finds the hidden child behind the green monster, and identifies with the pain that is inside him. Then all the anger subsides, he can trust, and he allows himself to fall into the arms of another. From that moment, the Hulk ceases to be an uncontrolled and incomprehensible part, and becomes part of the personality of the protagonist, who can choose to let it out or not.

Our internal monsters are often like wounded, angry children or teenagers rebelling against the world. They are pure pain, an infinite rage that has no end. If we know how to see through their behavior, all that they have broken, and the terrible things they have said to us, what these parts need most will come to pass. Someone will have realized how they feel, how much their life has hurt them, that they can't take it anymore. As soon as we understand this, even if all the sadness and suffering is still there, and even if there is still more anger than we would normally have now if faced with a similar situation, this part of us can now start playing on our side.

Most likely, when this starts to happen, we will notice it when we have to encounter someone we usually can't stand: our voice will come out stronger, with a conviction that is not our own. We can also see that we get angrier, more irritable, and that things that we previously overlooked now bother us. Those around us might not like these changes, and really this is not our final goal, but this more fluent connection with our previously dormant rage is a step forward when compared to the disconnection we come from. Now, joined with that part of ourselves, we feel stronger, at times we notice more energy, and we won't fall apart or get easily discouraged.

Since the reconciliation process has started, this part won't hate us as much as before. We won't feel rage towards ourselves for being weak, for submitting or for being wrong. When we get discouraged, we will no longer hear insults in our mind, but rather "Come on, wake up and go out and get some fresh air." We will also start seeing situations in a more nuanced way. We will be able to see both the pros and cons, take different aspects of a situation into account, and have a more complete vision of things, and this means we will make better decisions. We will no longer see this as something that is strange and unpleasant inside us, but as our own sensations; they will not yet be fully integrated, but they will begin to appear at the appropriate moments, take the correct direction, and start to come out.

The ghost that was able to rest

Some internal parts may be imbued with the spirit of certain figures in our lives. They reproduce the behaviors of people who have had great influence, power or control over us. In some way it's as if the influence of those people persists - even if they are no longer in our life or are not very close - by remaining present in our inner world and pointing out to us that, "They've not said their last word."

Our parents, teachers, or peers may have behaved towards us in such a pathological way that they completely altered our way of functioning. Their presence was so strong that they continue to be present in our minds, and their echo has persisted long afterwards. It's essential for us to go back and resolve our past with them, so the ghosts will stop interfering in our present life.

To do this, we have to sit in front of them and look directly at them. Like when we were children and we saw scary shadows, turning on the light makes many of them disappear and lets us see what they really represent. An alcoholic father who solved everything through violence is a sick person, incapable of managing his own life, and his opinion is probably the least authorized of any opinion that we know. The voice in our head insults us just like he did, repeating the phrases of a mad person blinded by alcohol, who did not know how to take care of himself or love his own family. These histories of alcohol and abuse often go back several generations, so, do we really want to continue that legacy? Our mind can learn from the best models. It's normal for us to repeat the old ones, but every time we hear our father's utterances in our head, we will stop to remember who is really speaking, and we will tell ourselves that we can learn to speak to ourselves differently.

We can help ourselves by doing an exercise to become aware of this. Let's imagine in our mind or draw on a piece of paper the part of ourselves that says to us what our father said, has impulses like his, and seems to replicate his behavior. Surely we don't want to be like that person, and seeing that image awakens the same fear and rejection that we felt before when we faced this person in the flesh and blood, this person we have copied those reactions from. Now let's take a real picture of that person or if we don't have one, imagine one. We will use the alcoholic father from the previous example. Let's stop calling him father and refer to him by his first name instead. Do not use the term "father" because an important moment of children's development is when they stop looking at their parents as symbolic figures, as the gods of their little world, and start to see them as real people. Therefore, we must try to look at the picture as if we were looking at an individual who is not related to us. What would we think of such a person? We would certainly see them as flawed, as a person with misguided beliefs, and as someone who is mentally unbalanced. We would see someone who has destroyed himself and those around him, and who continued to drink despite seeing how things got worse. We can see a person who never took responsibility for his actions and that, if at any time ever felt guilty about them, did nothing to rectify them. We can then imagine a conversation with the photo of our father, a conversation in which we tell him how he made us feel, how wrong he was, that he could not enjoy his family, that he never understood us at all, nor did he understand himself. We review how many opinions and perspectives on the world or ourselves he has transmitted to us, we tell him that this is his legacy, and then we refuse it. After all, his beliefs are just the opinions of an individual, and not exactly a wise one.

Apart from the instructions and rules imposed by that figure, his model contributed greatly to our learning of how to feel and regulate our emotions. When we felt bad, we saw his face filled with contempt. When we were scared in our room, we could hear him shouting in the background. The rage that the situation brought about turned into powerlessness, because we could never express our rage towards such an aggressive figure. We felt a lot of disgust and embarrassment at having been raised by a person like that. We say to the man in the photo that our emotions are good and that it makes sense to feel all these things, but now that we are adults, we can see everything from a very different point of view.

After doing this, we then turn to the part of us that imitates that model. We remind ourselves that the real person is one thing, but that we are now seeing a part of ourselves. We look at it again and observe what it looks like. Perhaps the realization that this part resembles our father, but is not our father, helps us to see it differently. Furthermore, to help this part evolve, we can use all the healthy models that we have ever known, from people who have valued us or who are able to express their rage with security and firmness while maintaining absolute respect for others. By looking at this part of ourselves as something different from the person it learned from, all the shame and disgust that we feel towards it will progressively become diluted, and we can start looking at it with acceptance and recognition. By doing this, the look on our father's face will disappear from the appearance of this internal part of us, his shape will change and be molded in a different way, and it will start to seem more and more like us.

This part must learn to be regulatory rather than destabilizing. This is normal at the beginning, because our part learned from a very dysregulated person. Now it can say different things to us when we are in different emotional states, and it can make comments that help, soothe, and soften our sensations. This part has incorporated other models, as it was not very difficult to find better models than our father's. This evolution takes time because we must overcome many fears and a lot of rejection towards ourselves. So, we need to have a lot of patience, because we know that it may take years to master a new language.

About when Miss Rottenmeier went to therapy and learned modern pedagogy

In the cartoon Heidi, Clara was the girl who Heidi went to live with for some time, and Miss Rottenmeier was Clara's severe, bitter governess. Miss Rottenmeier was an old-school governess, the daughter of a cold mother and an authoritarian, intransigent father, who had no point of reference on how to educate children other than her own parents. There was no place for games, joy or spontaneity, because they were things that had never been encouraged or allowed in her family. Heidi had indeed faced many hardships, but she had had an emotionally healthy caregiver because she lived for many years with a kind, loving grandfather. Clara had had no such luck. She had lost her mother, her father was both emotionally and physically absent, and she spent her childhood with her governess, a woman who was very limited by her own emotional needs. Clara's personality adapted; she became a timid girl with no spirit, who was blocked, even at a physical level, to the point of not being able to walk. The whole family changed with the arrival of Heidi, who brought in spontaneity, laughter and games. As a result, Clara's father became more emotionally present, and Miss Rottenmeier softened her character slightly. But let's go a little further.

Let's imagine that Miss Rottenmeier gets the chance to work on her personal story in psychotherapy and thus understands that she copied her parents' style because there was no other available to her. She realizes to what extent she did not have a real childhood and, little by little, she allows herself to change her perspective and points of view. She becomes aware that she now has sound points of reference on how to educate a child and begins her studies of pedagogy. There she discovers how wrong her educational methods are because punishment, whether physical or verbal, does not work to improve behavior. Although a person who gets punished may exhibit a change in the short term, eventually the person becomes more and more blocked, their self-esteem gets undermined and feelings of failure increase. If that blockage is met with more punishment, it grows even more.

Then Miss Rottenmeier discovers the importance of positive reinforcement. Giving a prize - emotional is better than material - a positive comment; paying attention to the behavior when a person is doing well; pointing out what part is correct, and when the person makes a mistake, congratulating them for the attempt and overlooking the result are all systems that promote improvement and effectiveness. When there are failures, focusing on them has no other consequence than increasing mistakes. Now, armed with this information, Miss Rottenmeier tries a new system with Clara and Heidi, and realizes how much they improve their functioning, and above all, their mood.

Our critical part may have evolved in a way that is similar to the governess in the story, and this part can learn the same way. We all need a critical part which helps us to recognize where we are wrong and push ourselves to improve. Without such a critical part, we would repeat the same mistakes without being aware of making them, and systematically do things wrong. We would not progress or evolve, and in addition we would have a very unrealistic picture of ourselves. Self-criticism is an essential part in all human beings, but if our part has learned from punitive, rigid and authoritarian teaching styles, it's important for us to understand why it acts this way and help it to try other more effective systems. When we realize that if we say, "What a mess! I'll have to do this again, I think that it would go better like this... Yes, that's better...! I'm learning, it's normal to make mistakes, I just need more practice," we will learn much better than if we tell ourselves, "I'm an idiot, everything I do is wrong, I'm worthless." Then our critical part will change its style and move towards the more effective one. By doing this, we are helping ourselves to unblock and better assimilate what happened to us in life and what we are going to experience in the future. We can see that our critical part is evolving when we start telling ourselves more productive and constructive things when we fail or have weaknesses.

When the Lost Boys returned from Neverland and finally grew up

Peter Pan and a group of boys lived in an imaginary, faraway place called Neverland, a place where time stood still, and the boys ceased to age upon arriving. In that land where time was frozen, nothing ever changed or evolved. Children came from complex families and troubled pasts, and in this place, they separated themselves from their reality. But over the years, Neverland became a prison for the children. Peter Pan, with his best intentions, had rescued them from their lives, but he did not know how to return them to reality. In addition, the circumstances that led the children to Neverland had changed, but for them, it was as if time hadn't passed.

Similarly, some experiences or life stages can get blocked in such a way that a part of us remains there and does not evolve like the rest of who we are. For example, if we were bullied at school, the frightened, humiliated child that we were then can stay within us, while we try to forget that stage. The same thing may happen to us in different situations. The sensitive child that no one understood hides within us, while we try to be strong and not show our feelings. The fussy, temperamental child who always insisted on having things their way to compensate for a lack of attention from their family disappeared inside after being chastised time and again, but our unmet needs for affection are still there, the same as when we were six. The teenager who did not feel that they belonged to any group or even to their own family, was getting covered up as we learned to charm people to ensure their presence in our life, but deep inside the feeling of not belonging is always there. It's as if those vulnerable, wounded or enraged children have never grown up, as if they continue living in Neverland, trapped in old memory networks to which all the new experiences of our lives, our good relationships, our successes, and our resources cannot reach.

The bridge that will make it so that these children can get unblocked and leave that place comes in the form of the adult that we are now, the adult that can see them with new eyes. From our present reality, we look at the children that we once were with understanding, and see the sensations that were brought on by what we lived through and the reactions that we were able to have, and those we couldn't have. If we look them in the eye, understand who they are, accept them along with everything they are carrying with them, understand what unmet needs they still have and look for a way to meet those needs in the present moment, networks of past and present memories will begin to connect and integrate. Then those children can evolve, grow, and develop to their full potential. The humiliated child will raise his head to realize that the school situation is over, and that he is an adult now who can protect himself. The sensitive child will discover that his emotions are good and that there are many people who he can share them with and who will value them. The fussy, temperamental child will start to become an adult who fights for what he wants in more pragmatic, reasonable, and effective ways, with the knowledge that it takes time to get things and requires making a directed effort towards it. The teenager will know that there are good things inside him and, recognizing how important it is to belong to something, will learn to connect with others in a more genuine way.

If we have difficulties as adults looking at our inner children with unconditional acceptance, we must ask ourselves if we are really looking at them with our own eyes, or are we still doing it through the eyes of the people we grew up with? If the latter is true, let's think about something: did we feel good when they looked at us like this? The answer is probably no, so we need to remember other people's ways of looking at us, the perspective of those who might have truly seen us, such as a teacher, a friend or a distant relative, even if it was only a little bit. Alternatively, we may consider how we would look at any child who was going through the same things and felt the same as we did. Keeping that child in mind, we can now look back at our inner child. Now we are really observing things from our own perspective. This change may take time, as it's common for our eyes to initially reflect what we learned in the past, and they have to go through a process of transformation. But it's important for us to work at this exercise regularly, because we really need to get our lost inner child back. Without them, we won't be complete, we won't be fully connected to our present experiences, and we won't fully enjoy things. It's important not to leave anything behind. Getting our inner child back does not mean that the painful sensations of those stages come to stay permanently; on the contrary, trying to leave them behind is precisely what makes these feelings remain within us forever. When the adult we are now embraces this child, the pain is relieved, the experience is integrated, and it gets resolved. The disturbing feelings dissolve in that hug, become scattered elsewhere in other memory networks, fade away and eventually disappear. Then we can truly move on and focus on our present reality.

22 THAT IS HOW THINGS WERE, THIS IS WHAT IT IS, AND THE FUTURE IS OPEN

Life can only be understood backwards, but it must be lived forwards.
Søren Kierkegaard.

Once we can go back through our history, we can begin to come to terms with it. We will be able to turn and face it without it hurting us, and without it conditioning our current life or our future. Of course, we draw lessons from the experience, but do not remain trapped by it or try to go in the opposite direction. We will be able to feel in the present[27], without re-experiencing old feelings or beliefs. From this new perspective, we won't see our future just as a repetition of what happened before; now we will know that it is open, and we are free to move in different directions. We will have gotten back our spontaneity and creativity.

Many therapeutic trends have pointed out the importance of acceptance in emotional well-being[28]. As we said, it's not possible to change a problem that we don't accept as being there. Acceptance does not mean resigning ourselves to our fate and doing nothing to change it. On the contrary, when we don't accept what comes in life, we have no capacity to modify our circumstances. We get stuck and stall if we do not take productive steps towards change.

This acceptance must extend to past and present situations, and our perspective on the future. Although in this book we are defending the importance of looking back to understand our history, this has nothing to do with repeating over and over in our head what happened to us and why. Just as analyzing the situations we experience is not the same as torturing ourselves internally with our bad luck, telling ourselves that this cannot be happening, or repeating "how can you do something like that?," or, "why does this happen?" The basis for change is to start reflecting on how we got here, what the situation is, and what options we have to modify it; but once all these aspects have been considered, we need to start working on possible solutions. To do so in an effective and realistic way, we must understand how the problem came to be, examine our present circumstances, and weigh up all the alternatives to change it, while fully accepting all these aspects. That's the way it was, this is what it is now, and let's see what we can do with we what have. That being said, let's get started and stop beating around the bush.

Trauma-oriented therapies point out the importance of integrating our history and the different parts of our personality that derive from it to prevent our forward-looking beliefs from being conditioned by that trauma. When we are able to do this, we'll be able to say, "This was my story. I can't change it, but I faced all those situations and I can completely assimilate them. I am now in the present, and I feel complete. I understand and accept all aspects of who I am. From this point, I can evolve and function differently in the future, without my past conditioning me in any way[29]."

Let's look at these three time frames - the past, the present, and the future - and see how we can learn to look at them from this perspective.

That's how things were

It may be that we haven't thought about our past in a long time or that we don't remember it, or that we have lived our life tortured by our memories, wondering why we ended up in these situations, or stuck on how unjust the world is. Either way, it doesn't matter, because our past has been conditioning our choices and relationships. If we have developed an awareness of this and have been making changes in the way we take care of ourselves, regulate ourselves and relate to others, it's time to rewrite our history. We can't change the facts, but we can develop a different interpretation of them. Our new narrative won't include guilt, pain, shame or bitterness. It does not mean that we must forgive others if they have hurt us, but it is important for us not to get trapped by anger, feel like we should have done something differently, or be mired in feelings of wanting revenge. We will have reached emotional distancing, or a certain indifference, which does not prevent us from knowing what is wrong is wrong and forming a negative moral judgment of the situations that deserve it. At this point we have already healed our wounds, sadness has been released and has left us, we have looked our shame in the face, and it has evaporated; disgust has been washed off our body, and our emotional blockage starts to lessen. We look at our past the same way we observe an old, faded photo, as something less vivid than reality. We remember what happened, but no longer feel sorry, not because we are disconnected from it, but because we are just over it. When we can look at an experience this way, it becomes just a memory - it's in the past.

We will do this going photo by photo, completing the album and organizing the facts. We will construct a new narrative of our life, as if we were editing a documentary in which we explain again how we got here. We will look at this story from a certain emotional distance. Although logically it makes us feel things and often affects us, it does not leave us indifferent, but it doesn't overwhelm us either.

We may have previously reviewed those moments, but it's useless to do this in despair or to ask ourselves, "How come I didn't do anything?" "How can people do these things?" or "Why do I have such bad luck?" These questions are not actually questions - they are traps. None of them allows us to accept that what happened just happened, and that there is no going back. Somehow, although we don't say it to ourselves this way, it's as if we wanted to take a time machine and go back to the past. But there is no such machine, and the past can't be changed. Whenever we say to ourselves, "If I'd done this… If I hadn't done that…" we are talking to ourselves as if there was still time to go back and change it, and this is impossible. Therefore, the only outcome of asking ourselves these questions is frustration and despair. Only by accepting the past as it was can we truly overcome it.

Accepting the past also means pushing doubts aside. When our memories are fuzzy or we are assailed by thoughts like, "I'm making this up," or "I'm making this out to be a much bigger deal than it really was," we lose focus and get distracted from what is most essential. Our memories are as they are, and it's true that the details may have not occurred as literally as we remember them, because the mind can alter memories based on other things that happened, or on what those around us did or said to us, as well as many other factors. But we are not conducting a police investigation, we are just trying to understand. Therefore, what matters to us is looking at memories as they are in our minds, because this is the information which is still influencing us. So, we shouldn't give it a further thought: this is how our memory stored the event, so this is the material we need to deal with. The essential thing is our subjective view, not so much the objective facts; what we need to assimilate is our experience, not the data. We are working on an emotional history, and some memories contain symbolic elements that are just as important as the literal details. Usually when we look at memories this way, caring more about our feelings than about investigating details, the situation will probably get clarified, the fog will dissipate, and after this, we will likely be more aware of how things really transpired.

Once we look back at our past, saying, "That's how it was, as I remember it, I did with it what I could," we are readier than ever to live our present without ties to the past. We have just learned from them).

This is what it is

As we move forward with getting beyond our past, we will see that we are more aware of the present. We will be able to accept things as they are now, without asking ourselves how things could have turned out differently if our past had been different. Then we would no longer live on the our imaginary world of dreams, inhabited by a modified version of the important people in our lives who are designed as we would like them to be, with everything we would like to have available to us. There is firm ground beneath our feet, and we will look for the things that we want. We know they are there, in different situations and in the people around us. They do not have that same shiny perfection as they did on our planet; they will be simpler and smaller, but also real. Once we have made peace with our past, we can also make peace with our reality.

The real world in the present is the only world that exists, and we should learn to navigate it. Although it sometimes seems like a world devastated by a storm, we can rebuild our house, sow new seeds, move to a new place or meet new people. This will be possible because we have regained the ability to explore, the desire to discover, and our curiosity. We won't do things like we always have. We will offer spontaneous and creative responses, even when situations repeat themselves. We are reinventing ourselves. But this should always happen based on our objective situation. This will be our starting point.

Saying, "This is what it is" has nothing to do with resignation and remaining stuck somewhere that we don't like - it has to do with acceptance. We can only modify something that we accept exists, and we will work to change only the part that can be changed, and not waste our energy trying to move a mountain that blocks the sun from shining on our house. We can learn to climb that mountain, go around it or use it as the subject of a painting; we can also sell the house and buy another one in a sunny place. In any case, we won't grow older in the same house, resenting the mountain for being there and lamenting our bad luck. We will accept that the mountain is there, make our decisions, and move towards achieving what we need.

Our future is open

The third step is the change in our perspective on the future. In many ways, a difficult past that we have not yet assimilated will condition our future. Beliefs that were generated in the past are likely to stay active, and we may still feel that we don't have control over our lives, that we have no options, that everyone will betray us or that we can't do anything. When we rewrite our history, we will also recover all our potential. We don't fight against ourselves, because all the different aspects of who we are belong to the same team. We have learned, and we will continue to learn, to protect ourselves and take care of ourselves. We are more open to others and choose more positive, supportive relationships. With all these resources, we will be more able to explore what is around us, and deal with whatever comes up.

During this process, we have been learning to enjoy uncertainty. So, when we say, "Let's wait and see," we are not afraid of the possibilities ahead; on the contrary, it will be a stimulating experience. Whatever comes will be new, and that is good, because we are clear about what is bad - even when it's well-known - it's just bad, and that doesn't interest us. Although we may feel a little anxious when faced with the unknown, we understand that it's normal and do not revert to the way we were. We take a risk, and go out and play. We already know that wounds heal and that we can get closure, that although we may hurt ourselves playing, we will recover. It's clear to us that living is worth it, with all its ups and downs.

This future that we envision is not a cliché, but rather a realistic picture that is constantly evolving and open to modification. We won't draw a bleak future for ourselves, one in which there is just "more of the same," a future in which we are doomed to give up everything that matters to us, a future with nothing on the horizon. Nor will we make a naive drawing, full of magic and things that are as wonderful as they are impossible. Our future must emerge from a perspective of what we want, a perspective that is perfectly viable - we must play the cards we have in our hand. We will set some goals, but we won't focus on them obsessively, and if necessary, we can revisit them as we go along, if circumstances change. We will put an address into our GPS and decide the route according to what we encounter along the way.

As we said, in order to consider the future from this open and free perspective, resolving the past is a must. For this journey, we need to cast off dead weight and keep only the things we have learned that are healthy. Perhaps we have to refuse legacies that are not in our interest to keep. Our feet must be securely planted in the present reality, firmly in contact with all our resources. Integrating the past and the present, and accepting every aspect of who we are, leaves us with endless possibilities as to what we can become.

23 THIS IS ME, THIS IS YOU, THIS IS US

A meeting of two: eye to eye, face to face. And when you are near I will tear your eyes out and place them instead of mine, and you will tear my eyes out and will place them instead of yours, then I will look at me with mine.
Jacob Levy Moreno.

Our identity - the way in which we see ourselves, others and relationships - will change as we go through the process. Our awareness of ourselves and the world is not something static, but is rather something that is in constant, dynamic change. We are not the same when we are babies as when we are teenagers or at any other life stages. Our perspective on what is around us also changes. As we mentioned, it's important not to cling to anything, but to let our awareness of things become fluid and be fed by the changes that we experience. Once we let go of our references, the new ones that replace them will get established in a natural way. Gradually, a clear vision of who we are, and what others are like, will emerge. We will still have points of reference, but these will become less fixed and external and more dynamic and internal. We will get our spontaneity and creativity back.

This is me

Learning from our history helps us understand ourselves in a more complete way. Those aspects of our personality that were incomprehensible make a lot of sense now in the light of the information that we have been assimilating. We have found the essence of every part of ourselves, and all of these parts have begun to evolve into new models. The fight with ourselves is over, and we have signed the peace treaty.

This does not mean that this process can ever be 100% complete. It's just that blockages are now cleared, everything begins to flow more easily, and we steer clear of difficulties. Although we handle our bike more easily, we might still fall off if we encounter a bump in the road. But now, we simply get up, check to make sure we're okay, bandage ourselves up if needed, and get back on the bike. Being okay and accepting ourselves as we are absolutely does not mean that we are perfect, that we will always feel happy or that nothing will ever trouble us.

As we have seen throughout this book, there are processes that need to be well-established so that the foundations of our structure will be solid. The way we take care of ourselves has improved, and doing what is good for us is now at the top of our list of priorities. Our emotional regulation system has to function by being aware of and tolerating our emotions, and not by trying to suppress or avoid them; this means listening to the needs each feeling represents, telling ourselves things that are useful for guiding and channeling our emotions, and modifying our perspective on situations so that we can see all the options available for dealing with them. We don't let our mind get trapped in false dilemmas between opposites, but rather we look for the middle ground between the extremes and search for intermediate solutions.

It's very possible that the old feelings will continue to rise up inside us, and that at times, old patterns will become active again. As we have explained throughout the book, if we spend years operating a certain way, this tendency does not disappear from one day to the next. But this doesn't mean that we are not going forward, because if we return to our recent learnings and resources as soon as possible, we will get back to the healthy route in no time. The more we stay on this path, the firmer our changes will be, making it more difficult for something to throw us off. This is what happens in normal development.

It's important for us to value just how significant these changes are, despite the ups and downs or the time it takes to regulate ourselves better. In bad moments, we can completely forget that we have made a lot of changes and that we have had much better days. For this reason, we must actively remind ourselves of this, so as to stay motivated throughout our process of change. That was how Destin was able to ride his bike with ease.

What is essential is that our functioning is not based on a fight against ourselves or a denial of our past or parts of our personality. Our energy is channeled towards a change that does not ignore the past, but instead sits on it so as to keep from repeating past problems. We already know that everything that is inside us can work in our favor. If we are still not clear on this, we must review our previous process, examine each urge and each aspect or part of ourselves again, and understand what is beneath it, and then rescue and embrace it. Everything that is in us needs to be accepted, and through this full acceptance, this can be transformed.

The process of re-integration of our personality is progressive and it will bring new sensations. We will feel more complete, but possibly more puzzled as well. The nuances of some experiences, which may have gone unnoticed and were associated with specific memories or parts, may start to get mixed up with other sensations. Our experiences will be far more nuanced than before, as if we are now painting with shades of different colors, instead of going from one very sharp emotion to another one that is also very clear and a polar opposite of the other. Learning to feel mixed emotions can be strange, but eventually it will become the normal way of feeling reality, and we will allow ourselves to have a closer understanding of it.

Sometimes there are aspects of our personality that we may want to keep pure. For example, we believe that if we quit our caregiver role, no one will love us, or if our controlling part is less present, we will fall into chaos. However, integrating such parts will allow us to take care of others in a more balanced way, and to exercise greater self-control. Our rage fusing with us will not imply that we will go back to being like the worst models that we know who expressed that emotion; on the contrary, when every last molecule in our body is in contact with our rage, we will feel it completely in our own way, noticing its firmness, security and force. Each part will be more present, and, at the same time, we will experience it in a completely different way. We will feel complete. We will know who we are.

This is you

The process of reconnecting with our experience and reconciling with ourselves also leads to a new vision of others. The way in which we were perceived or regarded by others in our earliest stages is how we learned to perceive ourselves. If no one really "saw" us or if they looked at us with rejection, hostility or criticism, this way of looking will shape the way in which we look at ourselves internally. But it will also mark our perspective towards what is around us, letting us easily project onto others what we saw so many times in the expression of those we grew up with. We may become hypersensitive to being disregarded, to any sign of rejection, hostility or criticism. We can detect these issues although they are minimal. At the same time, we may have difficulties perceiving positive attitudes. This way, we may amplify the effect of negative reactions in others or even understand many gestures as directed against us when they do not contain that intention. Many people who have experienced interpersonal traumas interpret neutral or even positive faces as loaded with negative emotions.

A second possibility is that we behave towards others as we were treated in the past. We look at the other person without really seeing who they are. We may reject their way of being, react aggressively toward them or harshly criticize others. We can be aware of it and, knowing how hard it was to experience these attitudes firsthand, we will feel terrible for doing it. There we can feel that "not me" of which we have spoken. A part of us that we reject takes control at that moment, and the more we reject that part, the more out of our control it becomes. It's also possible that we have no awareness of what we are doing or its meaning. By not having learned to look inwards with acceptance and understanding and reflect on what has happened to us, we might only see the final consequences of our actions, but not realize what our facial expressions look like, what gestures we make or what tone we use when we say things. If we are extremely upset, we might not even remember part of what we have said. Sometimes, literally, a piece of what has happened seems to be missing. We see that the other person reacts badly, and we become convinced that he reacted that way "just because;" without analyzing what happened in the moments leading up to it and what we said, we are satisfied with the simple explanation that "suddenly" the other person has attacked us because people are evil, or everybody treats us poorly. But when someone reacts badly to something that we say, our previous interaction with this person must have had something to do with it, and how the sequence unfolds will greatly influence how things turn out. To make changes, as we have said throughout this book, we must expand our awareness of ourselves. To do this, the reactions of others toward us will give us lots of interesting information, both positive and negative.

It's good for us to gain awareness of the influence that our past has on how we see others and assign meaning to their behavior. For example, we can be with a partner, but always see them as the person that will give us everything we have missed out on. We don't see the unique individual that we have in front of us, but the Prince Charming from our imaginary planet. Whenever the real being human we live with deviates from what we imagined, we feel bad or make them feel bad. Our eyes won't show acceptancc, but will instead show a flicker of criticism and disappointment, and this expression makes it very difficult for the other person to be receptive or willing to make the changes that we ask for.

Something similar may happen with other relationships. We look for extraordinary people, without the flaws that we all have, for people who will never fail us. For example, we hope that our parents, against all odds, stop behaving the way they always have. We don't see who they really are, and we resist accepting them and all their different layers. This is precisely what happened to us in our relationship with them, and strangely enough, we are repeating the same thing without realizing it.

Accepting others completely does not mean allowing them to harm us. In fact, understanding other people's characteristics helps us protect ourselves, because we don't deceive ourselves by thinking that people are just as we would like them to be, but instead, we actually see all their different aspects. Therefore, we can better calculate how we want to be in that relationship, what level of intimacy we want to have, and what we are and are not willing to tolerate.

This distorted view of the other, which is due to our own desires and ghosts, hinders the way in which we connect with others, even those we have strong and possibly positive ties with. For example, we can try to give our children everything we missed out on or protect them from the damage that we suffered. But they are new and different individuals, and they don't need what we didn't have - they just need what they need. We do not have to protect them from our past; we have to protect them from the world they live in.

We can also judge some people for the mistakes of others. If we had a violent father or husband, it's common for us to say to ourselves, "I don't want to have anything to do with men," which means painting an entire gender with the same brush, when in fact this conclusion is only appropriate for a specific person. The same happens if we were the victim of medical malpractice and afterwards, we no longer trust a single doctor; or if a girlfriend cheated on us and because of this, we conclude that all women are like that. If we grew up with a highly critical mother, we may react negatively when someone points out a mistake, even if they do so in a constructive manner. If our husband has been aggressive, then when our son has a tantrum - perhaps prompted by having witnessed his father's violent temper - we may stop seeing the child, and past traumatic memories with his father may come up to the surface.

All this can happen as a self-fulfilling prophecy. Previous beliefs which were established in significant relationships from the past make us detect the harmful elements of relationships in present situations and then amplify them. Every one of those details feeds back to our belief and makes us say, "You can't trust anybody!" or "It's clear that everybody is like that." For example, we may see rejection in the face of a coworker who greets us with an annoyed expression. He may look at everybody the same way, but we don't think "What happened to him?" Instead, we wonder, "Have I done something wrong?" or think "He doesn't like me." Our reaction to the look on his face, which will most likely not be to greet him as usual, will also influence him, and in turn, he may interpret our expression based on his own past. We function in some way as if we have telepathy and know with certainty why others do things, what they think, and how they feel, and usually assume that it has to do with us. We rely absolutely on our intuition. And while it's true that if we grew up or lived in a threatening environment, our sensors are very tuned to detect things that would slide right by others; it's also highly likely that we have a keener sense of identifying danger or harm than detecting other aspects of reality. In fact, when in doubt, we define many stimuli as dangerous or harmful when they are not. Just as we saw with John the solider, a highly sensitive danger detection system is a valuable resource in times of war, but it becomes a serious problem in times of peace. Our workmate may look like he's in a bad mood because he slept poorly, because his stomach aches, or he had an argument with his wife before leaving the house. Our colleague may have been raised by a very hostile mother and based on the prediction that he formed at that time, he feels that all people operate the same way. He is, in many ways, just like John the solider, a survivor of his own private war. Not everything has to do with us. Another possibility is that we project on to others what we don't like or can't accept about ourselves. We can see the rage that we hide inside ourselves in the face and attitudes of others, even when it's not what the other is really feeling. If we reject our anger to the point of not being aware at all that it is inside us, we can see only its reflection, even in people who are not showing it at all.

When our emotional disconnection is extreme, there can be a lot of deeply buried internal rage that permeates everything we do in a way that is so subtle that it is not evident to us or to others. Other people can react badly to this rage that seeps out of us, generating reactions that seem to come out of nowhere, and no one understands how or why. People may not want to be around us, but if we ask them why, they do not know and can't give us an "objective" reason. As mentioned, emotional disconnection takes its toll in many ways. It leaves us without keys to understanding reality and, above all, to understanding the complexity of our relationships with others.

We may also take for granted that what is in our mind is in other people's minds[30]. If we are upset, our prediction is that everyone else is upset too. If we grew up with caregivers who got readily caught up in our emotions, so much so that when we went home with a scraped knee, they would get more scared than we were, we may have learned that our emotions are always automatically in the minds of others. It's very likely that this happened to us, since it was the way of handling emotions that we learned from our first models. However, emotional regulation styles vary, and this emotional contagiousness does not occur in the majority of people. Others can feel very differently from what we are feeling, and think about what is happening in ways that we perhaps can't imagine. People are not clones, but rather beings with independent minds who follow their own processes. It's very important not to make simplistic explanations of human functioning. Our life experience is only a small fragment of reality. What happened in our family or in our significant relationships is not representative of the entire world. The rules governing these relationships do not work for everyone. If we always tend to interpret the functioning, the possible thoughts or the emotions of others in a very similar way, it's important for us to help ourselves break free from these mental frameworks. An exercise that can help us is to always think of five alternative explanations for someone else's behavior. That way, we get used to thinking that the other person "might" be upset with us, but that it might also be that his new shoes are bothering him, or his insurance company is refusing to pay for his car to be repaired. Our sensation will be very different when the worst possibility is not the only one that we can see.

Another aspect that can distort our interpretation of other people's behavior is that we relate an element of their character to others who have no connection to it. The characteristics of significant people in our life, both positive and negative, can get lumped together. For example, if our mother was messy, but positive and loving, our partner's tendency towards clutter may seem like an acceptable minor problem. On the other hand, if she was messy and abandoned us emotionally, clutter can become intolerable for us. The same thing may happen with positive traits. For example, if our mother was strict and demanding but did truly care for us, and after then she died and we were left in our grandparents' care, with whom we didn't feel important, being demanding will probably be a positive trait for us, and we will see it as a value in others. So sometimes we like or dislike characteristics in other people, not because they are good or bad in and of themselves, but - once again - because they are reminders of our past.

It would be useful, as mentioned above, to do the following reflection: as we are a product of our experiences, other people are the result of theirs as well. The reactions of others are conditioned by their learning and their circumstances. It's possible that part of what others feel about us actually has very little to do with us, but with their own experiences that connect in their mind in ways of which they are unaware. For example, if we have pointed out to a colleague that they have done something wrong, and he had a very harsh, critical mother, our comment will bother him greatly. His reaction has little to do with us in particular; his tolerance to criticism is very low because his system is hypersensitive to it. The more problematic, difficult or inadequate someone else's behavior is, the greater the likelihood that it is related to their own unresolved issues, since problematic behaviors are not characteristic of people who have formed healthy, enriching bonds. Most likely their interpretation of the world is distorted, they see enemies where there are none, and they are unrealistically judging their own behavior.

When our mind is freer of old patterns and our energy is not consumed by fighting against ourselves, we can look at other people from a new perspective. We will see others as autonomous beings, distinct from ourselves, with their own history and their own way of seeing the world. Now aware that we don't have true telepathy, we won't jump to conclusions or take anything for granted. For example, if our boss yells at us at work, we might think that his reaction may have something to do with us, but we will also consider other possible explanations. We don't think, "Why is he always after me?" or unconsciously associate his bad temper with the shouting in our family. On the contrary, we can say to ourselves things like, "This man has a self-control problem" or "What has gotten into him today?" This reflection in and of itself, which entails placing part of the problem on the other person's side, helps us to gain more emotional distance than thinking that it most certainly lies with us, and that everyone treats us badly. There could be many possible explanations; we don't have any information about the history of that person, but it is clear that his experiences have influenced how he understands and operates in the world. We may guess that perhaps he had demanding, authoritarian parents who influenced his personality, so we don't consider ourselves to be the only cause of his reaction, which can be magnified by his own internal process.

Once we reflect like this, we can think more calmly about whether or not we did something wrong. Perhaps we had a disagreeable look on our face without realizing it, or maybe we did indeed make a mistake. If we have practiced making mistakes a lot, and see them as something normal, we can admit that we are wrong without any problem. If we no longer criticize or blame ourselves internally too much, we can now be healthy and realistic when criticizing ourselves. If we don't do things well at work, it makes perfect sense for our boss to correct us. If he does it in a disproportionate or disrespectful way, that is indeed unacceptable, but that does not mean that we shouldn't assess ourselves and see if something needs changing. We review our behavior to see if we can identify any mistakes, and thanks to our healthy guilt, we recognize it, accept it and correct it. If we don't see that we have done anything inappropriate after a realistic analysis, we will be more capable of remaining calm even if he is still angry, because we have valued our opinion more than his. We don't take any of our ideas as indisputable, because we have learned not to fall for absolute certainties. We always think of various hypotheses to explain things, analyze the objective facts and draw conclusions with some degree of certainty when they are supported by facts, but we also keep our mind open to alternative explanations.

Facing and overcoming our past cleanses our mind of the residues from the past and allows us to see realistic pictures of the people around us. Accepting ourselves helps us to accept others. Having this perspective toward others has a great influence on our relationships with them, and makes it easier for these relationships to evolve in a positive way.

This is us

By seeing ourselves with all our nuances, distancing ourselves from our past without forgetting it, and understanding others as autonomous individuals, we get a very different way of functioning in relationships, a way that is freer, more spontaneous and more fluid. From this new position, an authentic encounter with another person is possible. We show them who we are and see the real person that we have in front of us. This meeting is one of those human experiences that is important not to miss, because they are the ones that make life worthwhile. Both fleeting moments with people we meet perhaps only once, and long-lasting relationships are experienced from a feeling of authenticity.

This connection is different from the intense bonding that we feel when we are still stuck in our memories. When we still have unmet needs for affection, we can see the same helplessness in the other person, the same frightened and vulnerable child we feel inside ourselves, and the same internal ghosts.

Strangely, not only what we feel internally, but even more what we don't accept about ourselves, is what powerfully attracts us to the other person. As we have forgotten to look inwards, these parts of us from which we are disconnected can become obvious only through the eyes of the other person. This feeling of being captivated can be labeled as "real" friendship or love, but it's really a symptom of our unresolved issues. Our rejected, ignored and wounded inner child is the one that gets hooked, and this happens on the fringes of our reasoning and awareness. The relationships based on these feelings tend to be full of anguish; they may activate our need to cling to others or to flee from intimacy, and they end up causing us suffering or pain again.

This, among others, is one of the reasons that makes us tend to get involved in pathological relationships repeatedly. This fact poses one of the most curious paradoxes that can lead us into traumatic situations. As much as we may try not to repeat an experience like the one we have gone through, we mysteriously end up with the same type of person or repeating similar situations. It's not our adult self who chooses partners or friends, but rather the inner child that we don't want to be. This inner child has never been able to learn from our past experiences and therefore still resides within us. Our unmet needs run rampant and seek out what is familiar to them. A person who was lucky enough to grow up in a healthy family environment and to have had more positive relationships won't have such marked deficiencies, and therefore we won't feel such a powerful connection to them. They may seem less "like us" or we think we don't care "enough." So we will tend to relate more to people who resonate with us, and with whom we also share similar problems.

A healthy encounter with another person is a more placid, solid, real feeling. It's also more durable, stable, and secure. When we make peace with all the aspects that form our personality and heal the wounds that our difficult memories have left us with, our way of being in the world and interacting with others will be different and more rewarding. It's clear that others can be in a different situation or stage and behave towards us in ways that are unhealthy, but our way of managing it will be more productive. We won't turn to others in search of protection and security, but with our own growing internal confidence, we will be able to establish ties of cooperation, understand other people and help them understand us. We will be able activate our own protection systems when required, but in the meantime, we won't feel that it's necessary.

All the changes that we have described in this book are possible for each and every one of us. Some will be easier than others, and many of them probably will take a lot of time, but achieving them depends only on how and how much we work in that direction. Like Destin and his bicycle, even the most deeply rooted patterns in our memory networks can be modified if we practice every day for the necessary amount of time. If we only read this book and think that some things make sense for us, but we don't work on them, it will end up being nothing more than an interesting reflection. Like the story of the boy and village, this book is just a handful of seeds. Let's reflect on what we want to do with them.

REFERENCES

1. This book seeks to offer an easily understood synthesis of theories of trauma, dissociation, attachment and emotional regulation and includes proposals and research on all these areas, which are too numerous to reference here. Selected books and authors have been included to clarify key concepts and provide suggestions for further, complementary reading.
2. Judith Herman defined the concept of complex PTSD in order to distinguish it from the post-traumatic stress that occurs following a single serious incident. The latest edition of her book is: *Trauma and Recovery. The Aftermath of Violence. From Domestic Abuse to Political Terror.* Basic Books, 2015
3. Bessel van der Kolk described the disorders of extreme stress, which are psychological reactions to serious and overwhelming life experiences, and the psychological consequences. One of his books is: *The Body Keeps the Score: Brain, Mind, and Body in the Healing of Trauma.* Penguin Books, 2015.
4. Jennifer Freyd (1998) proposed the idea that betrayal is the key element that makes an experience become traumatic, especially in the context of childhood. This author's theory is explained in *Betrayal Trauma: The Logic of Forgetting Childhood Abuse.* Harvard University Press, 1998.
5. Bureau, Martin, & Lyons-Ruth (2010). say that when we think of childhood trauma, it is common to relate it to physical or sexual abuse, and the feeling that our bodily integrity is threatened. However, the experience of threat is very different in children. Children trust that their caregivers will protect them and regulate their own emotions. When these caregivers are not available to do so, this gives rise to what are called hidden traumas, which are caused not so much by what happens, but by what is missing. These authores developed their ideas in a chapter (pp. 48-56) of the book *The Impact of Early Life Trauma on Health and Disease: The Hidden Epidemic*, Cambridge University Press, edited by Lanius, Vermetten, & Pain.

6. Martin Teicher is a researcher who has analyzed the influence of various types of trauma on the development of the nervous system. Experiences can impact us in different ways depending on the stage in which each type of experience occurs. These experiences can influence how our personality develops, and later contribute to the appearance of various types of psychological problems. (See for example Schalinski, Teicher, Nischk, Hinderer, Muller, & Rockstroh, 2016. Type and timing of adverse childhood experiences differentially affect severity of PTSD, dissociative and depressive symptoms in adult inpatients. *BMC Psychiatry*, 16).
7. The European Association of Trauma and Dissociation (ESTD) brings together professionals interested in these disorders and provides resources for their understanding and treatment (www.estd.org). Another association with similar aims is the ISSTD (International Society for the Study of Trauma and Dissociation: www.isst-d.org). There are also two speciliazed journals: The *Journal of Trauma and Dissociation* and the *European Journal of Trauma and Dissociation.*
8. Giovanni Liotti has studied disorganized attachment styles and their relationship with mental fragmentation and dissociation of personality. He also defined the so-called controlling strategies, in which aggression against caregivers or caring for caregives are substitutes for bonds of attachment (Liotti, 2009: Attachment and dissociation. In the book by Dell and O'Neil: *Dissociation and the Dissociative Disorders: DSM-V and Beyond*, Routledge, 2009.
9. This article describes how the losses suffered by a mother in the first two years after the birth of a child may affect the bonds of attachment. Liotti & Pasquini, 2000: Predictive factors for borderline personality disorder: Patients' early traumatic experiences and losses suffered by the attachment figure. *Acta Psychiatrica Scandinavica*, 102, 4: 282-289.
10. James Gross has extensively revised the processes of emotional regulation, especially with regard to the cognitive control of emotions. The situations that generate emotions, and what we do with them, condition how our emotional state is resolved. According to the author, the healthiest thing is to carefully choose the situation that we find ourselves in, decide how long we are going to stay there, and once this emotion is activated, without trying to avoid or repress it, reformulate it to see it from the most

helpful perspective. A good deal of research about emotional regulation has been conducted and many texts have been written about this developing field in neuroscience and psychotherapy. *Handbook of Emotion Regulation.* Guilford Press, 2015.

11. Jeffrey Young developed schema therapy, based on the understanding of the different mental states from which we operate and their origins in our life experiences. These experiences mostly occur in childhood. Although the states described here are not the same, the basic idea is similar. *Reinventing Your Life: How to Break Free from Negative Life Patterns and Feel Good*, Penguin, 2009.
12. Stephen Porge's fundamental articles are included in the book: *The Polyvagal Theory: Neurophysiological Foundations of Emotions, Attachment, Communication, and Self-regulation.* Norton, 2011.
13. In an interesting and easy-to-read book, Jo Marchant reviews how body and mind can influence each other: *Cure: A Journey into the Science of Mind over Body*, Broadbooks, 2017.
14. HRV stands for Hearth Rate Variability. A compilation of the research on HRV and its clinical applications can be found in Donald Moss and Fred Schaffer's book: *Biofeedback. Applied Psychophysiology and Biofeedback*, AAPB, 2004.
15. The ACE (Adverse Childhood Experiences) study analyzed how having faced different adversities in childhood or adolescence (physical, emotional or sexual abuse, abandonment, loss, witnessing violence towards the mother, living with a person with alcoholism, drug addiction or mental illness or someone in the family who committed suicide or is incarcerated) may influence our mental state. The results of this study have given rise to numerous scientific publications which show the cumulative effect of these experiences on the development of very diverse types of psychiatric and somatic disorders. Bellis, et al. (2017). The impact of adverse childhood experiences on health service use across the life course using a retrospective cohort study. *Journal of Health Services Research & Policy*, 22, 3: 168-177.
16. Daniel Siegel (2012) beautifully explains the relationship between caregiver-child interactions and the emotional development of the brain in his book: The Whole-Brain Child: 12 Revolutionary Strategies to Nurture Your Child's Developing Mind,Random House. An easy to read book about how emotional regulation is

learned.

17. Mary Main and Judith Solomon defined a subtype of attachment disturbance called disorganization. Main says that disorganized attachment derives from the perception of the attachment figure as frightening or frightened. This behavior happens unexpectedly in caregivers due to their internal triggers, and its unexplained nature will alarm the child. The caregiving figure will be the place to look for protection and the place from which the alarm that triggered the system of attachment comes (Main & Solomon (1986) Discovery of a new, insecure-disorganized/disoriented attachment pattern. In *Yogman & Brazelton, Affective development in infancy*, p 95-124. Ablex). See also Main & Hesse (1990) Parent's unresolved traumatic experiences are related to infant disorganized attachment status: Is frightened and/or frightening parental behavior the linking mechanism? In Greenberg, Chicchetti & Cummings (Eds) *Attachment in the preschool years: Theory, research and intervention*, 161-182. University of Chicago Press.

18. Onno van der Hart, Ellert Nijenhuis, and Kathy Steele, defined the concept of structural dissociation of the personality to describe this fragmentation. They also point out the importance of the realization of what has happened to us and its influence on our present functioning, in order to get rid of it and face the future differently. Their reference book is: *The Haunted Self. Structural Dissociation and the Treatment of Chronic Traumatization.* Norton, 2006.

19. Cognitive-analytic psychotherapy is a synthesis between psychodynamic theories, coming from psychoanalysis, and cognitive therapy. One concept in this approach is understanding problems as traps (solutions that complicate things more), dilemmas (false choices between opposites) and snags (things that take us back when we try to improve). Another interesting concept in this therapy is how our mental state triggers a complementary response in the other, sometimes getting into relational loops (reciprocal roles). A book for professionals on this approach is that of Anthony Ryle and Ian Kerr (2001). *Introduction to Cognitive-Analytic Therapy: Principles and Practice.* Wiley.

20. Seligman (1975) defined the phenomenon of learned helplessness. It was initially described in animals that had to repeatedly confront painful or negative stimuli which could not be avoided. After this

experience, the body does not know how to resort to escape or avoidance in new situations in which it would be possible and effective. They learn that the negative stimulus has to be accepted, that they have lost control and give up even before attempting to escape. This reaction has been associated with depression and other mental disorders (*Helplessness: On Depression, Development, and Death.* Freeman/Times Books).

21. In www.smartereveryday.com this engineer explores the world using science, and presents new perspectives on things.
22. Lerner (1980) defined what he called the just-world hypothesis. In line with this hypothesis, people need to believe (against the overwhelming available evidence) that the world is fair, that there is an order to it, and that people often get what they deserve. When there is injustice, people try to help the victim to restore that order, and when this is not possible, they blame the victim. Assuming that things do not follow any rules, and that we have no control over them, results in an intolerable cognitive dissonance. *The Belief in a Just World: A Fundamental Delusion.* Plenum Press.
23. Marsha Linehan (2014) has developed the so-called dialectic behavioral therapy for the treatment of borderline personality disorder, characterized, among other features, by emotional instability and a tendency toward extreme reactions. This therapy has been used subsequently for other problems. One of the main areas of this psychotherapy is working on polarized reactions, striking a balance between the radical acceptance of self and reality, and the commitment to change toward health. *DBT Skills Training Manual.* The Gilford Press.
24. Smith (1981) proposed a simple guide on how to be more assertive, how to say no without giving in, and how to respond to criticism and to manipulation. From our book's perspective, his book states a way of expressing rage between the uncontrolled explosion and containment and submission. *When I Say No, I Feel Guilty.* Random House.
25. EMDR is a type of psychotherapy developed over the last several decades by Francine Shapiro. It has been recognized by the World Health Organization as an evidence-based therapy to treat post-traumatic stress. To understand how EMDR works and it

neurobiological basis, a good book is: *Getting Past your Past*, Rodale Books, 2013. More information about EMDR can be found on the EMDR Institute's website (www.emdr.org), which includes a large number of scientific studies supporting the efficacy of this psychotherapy.

26. The analysis of different treatments shows that therapies designed to specifically work with problems arising from traumatic experiences work better than generic therapies that do not focus on this area. Ehlers et al., (2010.). Do all psychological treatments really work the same in posttraumatic stress disorder? *Clinical Psychology Review*, 30, 2: 269-276.
27. In recent years mindfulness techniques have become increasingly popular but have also been trivialized. Their basic elements are acceptance, self-awareness and compassion. Self-awareness helps us to live in the present and observe the moment in depth. Compassion is a way of looking at ourselves and the world that surrounds us. An introduction to the subject written by Jon Kabat-Zinn is: *Mindfulness for Beginners: Reclaiming the Present Moment and Your Life.* Sounds True, 2016.
28. Acceptance and commitment therapy is one of the so-called third-generation therapies, derived from cognitive-behavioral therapy. This theapeutic approach analyzes what factors are related to change in psychotherapy, in essence, what is it that makes some people change and others not? According to what this approach proposes, suffering is something that goes far beyond the emotions generated by situations in life. If we lose someone, we feel bad, but if we blame ourselves for what we did not do, we add more suffering on top of what happen. The elements that hinder change are (1) not accepting things as they are, (2) not engaging in the process of change and (3) our dysfunctional beliefs.. An introductory book is: Hayes (2005). *Get Out of Your Mind and Into Your Life: The New Acceptance and Commitment Therapy.* New Harbinger.
29. In addition to *The Haunted Self*, which has been previously mentioned, Suzette Boon and Kathy Steele have published a more practical and patient-oriented manual: *Coping with Trauma-Related Dissociation: Skills Training for Patients and Therapists.* Norton, 2015.
30. Antony Bateman and Peter Fonagy have developed a

mentalization-based therapy that is rooted in the psychoanalytic approach and closely related to attachment theories. The authors point out that we can only learn to get perspective on our mental processes and see the mind of others as something distinct from our mind, if our first relationships were based on a healthy form of bonding. When caregivers realized how we felt, they mirrored our mental states, and understood our mind as different from theirs; later we internalized these relationship models with ourselves and when we interacted with others. This awareness ability can be trained through the psychotherapeutic process. *Mentalization Based Treatment for Personality Disorders: A Practical Guide.* Oxford University Press, 2016.

ABOUT THE AUTHOR

Anabel Gonzalez is a psychiatrist and psychotherapist who has trained in various therapeutic approaches such as Group Therapy, Cognitive Analytic Therapy, Systemic Therapy and trauma-oriented therapies. She holds a PhD in Medicine and is a specialist in Criminology. She belongs to the Board of the European Society for Trauma and Dissociation (ESTD) and is Vice President of the EMDR Spanish Association. She works at the University Hospital of A Coruña (CHUAC), where she coordinates the Trauma and Dissociation Program which focuses on patients with severe traumatization. She is actively lectures and giving training on dissociative disorders, trauma, attachment and emotional regulation, as well as being an accredited EDMR therapy trainer. She is a teaching collaborator in her hospital, where she coordinates psychotherapy training for psychiatry residents. She has participated as a guest lecturer in the Master's in EMDR Therapy at the Universidad Nacional de Educación a Distancia (UNED). At the research level, she directs several projects in the field of trauma and treatment with EMDR for various disorders. She has published numerous articles on dissociation, trauma and EMDR, and is author/co-author of the books *Trastornos Disociativos* and *Trastorno de Identidad Disociativo* (only in Spanish) and *EMDR and Dissociation, the Progressive Approach*, and *EMDR and BPD*.

www.anabelgonzalez.es

Other books by the author

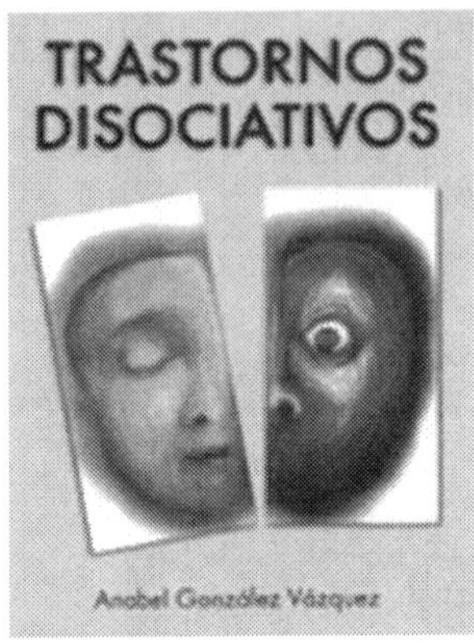

Trastornos disociativos. *Anabel Gonzalez (2013). Ed. Pléyades.*

Dissociative disorders are common clinical pictures, but often go unnoticed due to the mix of symptoms that they present. Their treatment requires a specific methodology, including addressing the mental fragmentation that these conditions present. This book describes their origin, characteristics, and treatment in a practical way.

EMDR and Dissociation: the Progressive Approach. *Anabel Gonzalez and Dolores Mosquera (2013).*

EMDR therapy is an evidence-based treatment for PTSD which requires adaptations when applied in more complex post-traumatic conditions, particularly in dissociative disorders. This is a book for therapists trained in EMDR that describes procedures for working with this psychotherapy in severe post-traumatic conditions.

Borderline Personality Disorder and EMDR Therapy. *Dolores Mosquera and Anabel Gonzalez (2014). Ed. Pléyades.*

Borderline Personality Disorder calls for an integrative approach, which includes the treatment of early attachment problems and the traumatic history often associated with this condition. EMDR work focuses on these areas, covering aspects such as self-care, emotional regulation, and interpersonal problems.

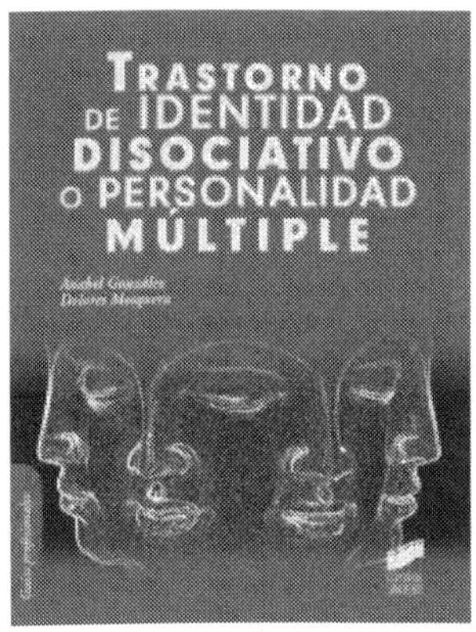

Trastorno de identidad disociativo o personalidad múltiple. *Anabel Gonzalez y Dolores Mosquera (2015). Ed. Síntesis.*

Dissociative identity disorder, formerly known as multiple personality disorder, is the most severe condition in the dissociative disorders group. According to prevalence studies in different countries, around 5% of patients in the care of mental health services would receive this diagnosis. The text goes through the triggering factors, clinical features and specific therapeutic strategies.

Made in the USA
Las Vegas, NV
10 November 2021